LEARN TO SPEAK CHINESE FROM ENGLISH

THE ART OF SPEAKING CHINESE FROM ENGLISH

RANJAN BARMAN

ISBN 979-888546993-7

Learn to speak Chinese from English

Author: Ranjan Barman

FIRST EDITION 2022

blograter.com

MRP: 499 INR

Dedication:

To my parents, brother, wife & son

About The Book

This book will help you speak Chinese directly from English language. This book will not teach you about Chinese alphabates. If you only want to know the way to speak Chinese from English then this is the perfect book for you.

I have provided video tutorial link at the end of page that will help you learn Chinese pronunciation.

The symbols you will see over the English alphabets those are tones. You will learn about them in the video tutorial. The link I have provided at the last page of this book.

I have used very simple sequence of English sentences and their Chinese translation. You need to keep reading the sentences and practice it. You will find the logic of Chinese sentence making structures.

Contents

CHAPTER ONE

Chapter 1

1 I do. Wǒ zuò. 我做。
2 I am doing. Wǒ zài zuò. 我在做。
3 I have done. Wǒ yǐjīng zuò hǎole. 我已经做好了。
4 I did. Wǒ zuò dàole. 我做到了。
5 I was doing. Wǒ zài zuò. 我在做。
6 I will do. Wǒ huì zuò. 我会做。
7 I will be doing. Wǒ huì zuò de. 我会做的。
8 I will have done. Wǒ huì zuò dào de. 我会做到的。
9 I can do. Wǒ kěyǐ. 我可以。
10 I could do. Wǒ kěyǐ zuò. 我可以做。
1 I do. Wǒ zuò. 我做。
2 We do. Wǒmen díquè shì. 我们的确是。
3 You do. Nǐ zuò. 你做。
4 You do. Nǐ zuò. 你做。
5 He does. Tā shì zhèyàng de. 他是这样的。
6 She does. Tā huì. 她会。
7 It does. Quèshí rúcǐ. 确实如此。
8 Ridhaan does. Lǐ dá ēn kěyǐ. 里达恩可以。
9 They do. Tāmen shì zhèyàng. 他们是这样。
10 Children do. Háizimen zuò. 孩子们做。
1 I am doing. Wǒ zài zuò. 我在做。
2 We are doing. Wǒmen zhèngzài zuò. 我们正在做。
3 You are doing. Nǐ zài zuò. 你在做。
4 You are doing. Nǐ zài zuò. 你在做。
5 He is doing. Tā zài zuò. 他在做。
6 She is doing. Tā zài zuò. 她在做。
7 It is doing. Tā zhèngzài zuò. 它正在做。
8 Ridhaan is doing. Ridhaan zhèngzài zuò. Ridhaan正在做。

9 They are doing. Tāmen zài. 他们在。

10 Children are doing. Háizimen zài zuò. 孩子们在做。

1 I have done. Wǒ yǐjīng zuò hǎole. 我已经做好了。

2 We have done. Wǒmen yǐjīng zuò dàole. 我们已经做到了。

3 You have done. Nǐ yǐjīng wánchéngle. 你已经完成了。

4 You have done. Nǐ yǐjīng wánchéngle. 你已经完成了。

5 He has done. Tā wánchéngle. 他完成了。

6 She has done. Tā zuò dàole. 她做到了。

7 It has done. Tā yǐjīng zuò dàole. 它已经做到了。

8 Ridhaan has done. Ridhaan zuò dàole. Ridhaan 做到了。

9 They have done. Tāmen yǐjīng zuò dàole. 他们已经做到了。

10 Children have done. Háizimen zuò dàole. 孩子们做到了。

1 I did. Wǒ zuò dàole. 我做到了。

2 We did. Wǒmen zuò dàole. 我们做到了。

3 You did. Nǐ zuò dàole. 你做到了。

4 You did. Nǐ zuò dàole. 你做到了。

5 He did. Tā zuò dàole. 他做到了。

6 She did. Tā zuòguò. 她做过。

7 It did. Tā zuòle. 它做了。

8 Ridhaan did. Ruì dān zuò dàole. 瑞丹做到了。

9 They did. Tāmen zuò dàole. 他们做到了。

10 Children did. Háizimen zuò dàole. 孩子们做到了。

1 I was doing. Wǒ zài zuò. 我在做。

2 We were doing. Wǒmen zài zuò. 我们在做。

3 You were doing. Nǐ zài zuò. 你在做。

4 You were doing. Nǐ zài zuò. 你在做。

5 He was doing. Tā zài zuò. 他在做。

6 She was doing. Tā zài zuò. 她在做。

7 It was doing. Tā zài zuò. 它在做。

8 Ridhaan was doing. Ridhaan zhèngzài zuò. Ridhaan正在做。

9 They were doing. Tāmen zài zuò. 他们在做。

10 Children were doing. Háizimen zài zuò. 孩子们在做。

1 I will do. Wǒ huì zuò. 我会做。

2 We will do. Wǒmen huì zuò de. 我们会做的。

3 You will do. Nǐ huì qù zuò de. 你会去做的。

4 You will do. Nǐ huì qù zuò de. 你会去做的。

5 He will do. Tā huì zuò de. 他会做的。

6 She will do. Tā huì zuò de. 她会做的。

7 It will do. Tā huì zuò. 它会做。

8 Ridhaan will do. Ridhaan huì zuò de. Ridhaan会做的。

9 They will do. Tāmen huì zuò de. 他们会做的。

10 Children will do. Háizimen huì zuò de. 孩子们会做的。

1 I will be doing. Wǒ huì zuò de. 我会做的。

2 We will be doing. Wǒmen huì zuò de. 我们会做的。

3 You will be doing. Nǐ huì zuò de. 你会做的。

4 You will be doing. Nǐ huì zuò de. 你会做的。

5 He will be doing. Tā huì zuò de. 他会做的。

6 She will be doing. Tā huì zuò de. 她会做的。

7 It will be doing. Tā huì zuò. 它会做。

8 Ridhaan will be doing. Ridhaan huì zuò de. Ridhaan 会做的。

9 They will be doing Tāmen huì zuò 他们会做

10 Children will be doing. háizimen huì zuò de. 孩子们会做的。

1 I will have done. Wǒ huì zuò dào de. 我会做到的。

2 We will have done. Wǒmen huì zuò dào de. 我们会做到的。

3 You will have done. Nǐ huì zuò dào de. 你会做到的。

4 You will have done. Nǐ huì zuò dào de. 你会做到的。

5 He will have done. Tā huì zuò dào de. 他会做到的。

6 She will have done. Tā huì zuò dào de. 她会做到的。

7 It will have done. Tā huì zuò dào de. 它会做到的。

8 Ridhaan will have done. Ridhaan huì zuò dào de. Ridhaan会做到的。

9 They will have done. Tāmen huì zuò dào de. 他们会做到的。

10 Children will have done. Háizimen huì zuò dào de. 孩子们会做到的。

1 I can do. Wǒ kěyǐ. 我可以。

2 We can do. Wǒmen néng zuò de. 我们能做的。

3 You can do. Nǐ kěyǐ zuò. 你可以做。

4 You can do. Nǐ kěyǐ zuò. 你可以做。

5 He can do. Tā kěyǐ. 他可以。

6 She can do. Tā kěyǐ. 她可以。

7 It can do. Tā kěyǐ zuò dào. 它可以做到。

8 Ridhaan can do. Ridhaan kěyǐ. Ridhaan 可以。

9 They can do. Tāmen kěyǐ. 他们可以。

10 Children can do. Hái zǐ kěyǐ zuò. 孩子可以做。

1 I could do. Wǒ kěyǐ zuò. 我可以做。

2 We could do. Wǒmen kěyǐ. 我们可以。

3 You could do. Nǐ kěyǐ. 你可以。

4 You could do. Nǐ kěyǐ. 你可以。

5 He could do. Tā kěyǐ. 他可以。

6 She could do. Tā kěyǐ. 她可以。

7 It could do. Tā kěyǐ zuò dào. 它可以做到。

8 Ridhaan could do. Ridhaan kěyǐ. Ridhaan 可以。

9 They could do. Tāmen kěyǐ. 他们可以。

10 Children could do. Háizi men kěyǐ. 孩子们可以。

1 I don’t do. Wǒ bù zuò. 我不做。

2 We don’t do. Wǒmen bù zuò. 我们不做。

3 You don’t do. Nǐ bù zhèyàng zuò. 你不这样做。

4 You don’t do. Nǐ bù zhèyàng zuò. 你不这样做。

5 He doesn’t do. Tā bù zuò. 他不做。

6 She doesn’t do. Tā bù zuò. 她不做。

7 It doesn’t do. Bùxíng. 不行。

8 Ridhaan doesn’t do. Ridhaan bù zhèyàng zuò. Ridhaan 不这样做。

9 They don’t do. Tāmen bù zhèyàng zuò. 他们不这样做。

10 Children don’t do. Háizimen bù zhèyàng zuò. 孩子们不这样做。

1 I am not doing. Wǒ bùshì zài zuò. 我不是在做。

2 We are not doing. Wǒmen bùshì zài zuò. 我们不是在做。

3 You are not doing. Nǐ bùshì zài zuò. 你不是在做。

4 You are not doing. Nǐ bùshì zài zuò. 你不是在做。

5 He is not doing. Tā bùshì zài zuò. 他不是在做。

6 She is not doing. Tā bùshì zài zuò. 她不是在做。

7 It is not doing. Tā bùshì zài zuò. 它不是在做。

8 Ridhaan is not doing. Ridhaan méiyǒu zuò. Ridhaan 没有做。

9 They are not doing. Tāmen bùshì zài zuò. 他们不是在做。

10 Children are not doing. Háizi bù gān. 孩子不干。

1 I have not done. Wǒ méiyǒu zuòguò. 我没有做过。

2 We have not done. Wǒmen hái méiyǒu zuò dào. 我们还没有做到。

3 You have not done. Nǐ hái méiyǒu zuò. 你还没有做。

4 You have not done. Nǐ hái méiyǒu zuò. 你还没有做。

5 He has not done. Tā hái méiyǒu zuò dào. 他还没有做到。

6 She has not done. Tā méiyǒu zuòguò. 她没有做过。

7 It has not done. Tā méiyǒu zuò dào. 它没有做到。

8 Ridhaan has not done. Ridhaan méiyǒu zuò. Ridhaan 没有做。

9 They have not done. Tāmen hái méiyǒu zuò dào. 他们还没有做到。

10 Children have not done. Háizi méi zuòguò. 孩子没做过。

1 I did not do. Wǒ méiyǒu zuò. 我没有做。

2 We did not do. Wǒmen méiyǒu zuò. 我们没有做。

3 You did not do. Nǐ méiyǒu zuò. 你没有做。

4 You did not do. Nǐ méiyǒu zuò. 你没有做。

5 He did not do. Tā méiyǒu zuò. 他没有做。

6 She did not do. Tā méiyǒu zuò. 她没有做。

7 It did not do. Tā méiyǒu zuò. 它没有做。

8 Ridhaan did not do. Ridhaan méiyǒu zhèyàng zuò. Ridhaan没有这样做。

9 They did not do. Tāmen méiyǒu zhèyàng zuò. 他们没有这样做。

10 Children did not do. Háizi méiyǒu zuò. 孩子没有做。

1 I was not doing. Wǒ bùshì zài zuò. 我不是在做。

2 We were not doing. Wǒmen bùshì zài zuò. 我们不是在做。

3 You were not doing. Nǐ bùshì zài zuò. 你不是在做。

4 You were not doing. Nǐ bùshì zài zuò. 你不是在做。

5 He was not doing. Tā bùshì zài zuò. 他不是在做。

6 She was not doing. Tā bùshì zài zuò. 她不是在做。

7 It was not doing. Tā bùshì zài zuò. 它不是在做。

8 Ridhaan was not doing. Ridhaan méiyǒu zuò. Ridhaan 没有做。

9 They were not doing. Tāmen méiyǒu zuò. 他们没有做。

10 Children were not doing. Háizimen méiyǒu zuò. 孩子们没有做。

1 I will not do. Wǒ bù huì. 我不会。

2 We will not do. Wǒmen bù huì zuò. 我们不会做。

3 You will not do. Nǐ bù huì zuò de. 你不会做的。

4 You will not do. Nǐ bù huì zuò de. 你不会做的。

5 He will not do. Tā bù huì zuò de. 他不会做的。

6 She will not do. Tā bù huì zuò de. 她不会做的。

7 It will not do. Tā bù huì zuò. 它不会做。

8 Ridhaan will not do. Ridhaan bù huì. Ridhaan 不会。

9 They will not do. Tāmen bù huì zuò de. 他们不会做的。

10 Children will not do. Háizi bù huì zuò. 孩子不会做。

1 I will not be doing. Wǒ bù huì zuò de. 我不会做的。

2 We will not be doing. Wǒmen bù huì zuò. 我们不会做。

3 You will not be doing. Nǐ bù huì zuò de. 你不会做的。

4 You will not be doing. Nǐ bù huì zuò de. 你不会做的。

5 He will not be doing. Tā bù huì zuò de. 他不会做的。

6 She will not be doing. Tā bù huì zuò de. 她不会做的。

7 It will not be doing. Tā bù huì zuò. 它不会做。

8 Ridhaan wil not l be doing. Ridhaan wǒ bù huì zuò de. Ridhaan 我不会做的。

9 They will not be doing. Tāmen bù huì zuò de. 他们不会做的。

10 Children will not be doing. Háizi bù huì zuò. 孩子不会做。

1 I will not have done. Wǒ bù huì zuò de. 我不会做的。

2 We will not have done. Wǒmen bù huì zuò. 我们不会做。

3 You will not have done. Nǐ bù huì zuò de. 你不会做的。

4 You will not have done. Nǐ bù huì zuò de. 你不会做的。

5 He will not have done. Tā bù huì zuò de. 他不会做的。

6 She will not have done. Tā bù huì zuò de. 她不会做的。

7 It will not have done. Tā bù huì wánchéng. 它不会完成。

8 Ridhaan will not have done. Ridhaan bù huì zhèyàng zuò. Ridhaan 不会这样做。

9 They will not have done. Tāmen bù huì zuò de. 他们不会做的。

10 Children will not have done. Háizimen bù huì zuò de. 孩子们不会做的。

1 I can not do. Wǒ bùnéng zuò. 我不能做。

2 We can not do. Wǒmen zuò bù dào. 我们做不到。

3 You can not do. Nǐ zuò bù dào. 你做不到。

4 You can not do. Nǐ zuò bù dào. 你做不到。

5 He can not do. Tā zuò bù dào. 他做不到。

6 She can not do. Tā zuò bù dào. 她做不到。

7 It can not do. Tā zuò bù dào. 它做不到。

8 Ridhaan can not do. Ridhaan zuò bù dào. Ridhaan做不到。

9 They can not do. Tāmen zuò bù dào. 他们做不到。

10 Children can not do. Háizi zuò bù dào. 孩子做不到。

1 I could not do. Wǒ zuò bù dào. 我做不到。

2 We could not do. Wǒmen zuò bù dào. 我们做不到。

3 You could not do. Nǐ zuò bù dào. 你做不到。

4 You could not do. Nǐ zuò bù dào. 你做不到。

5 He could not do. Tā zuò bù dào. 他做不到。

6 She could not do. Tā zuò bù dào. 她做不到。

7 It could not do. Tā zuò bù dào. 它做不到。

8 Ridhaan could not do. Ridhaan zuò bù dào. Ridhaan 做不到。

9 They could not do. Tāmen zuò bù dào. 他们做不到。

10 Children could not do. Háizimen zuò bù dào. 孩子们做不到。

1 Do I do?. Wǒ zuò ma?. 我做吗？。

2 Do we do?. Wǒmen zuò ma? 我们做吗？

3 Do you do?. Nǐ zuò ma? 你做吗？

4 Do you do?. Nǐ zuò ma? 你做吗？

5 Does he do?. Tā zuò ma?. 他做吗？。

6 Does she do?. Tā zuò ma?. 她做吗？。

7 Does it do?. Xíng ma?. 行吗？。

8 Does Ridhaan do?. Ridhaan yǒu ma? Ridhaan 有吗？

9 Do they do?. Tāmen zuò ma? 他们做吗？

10 Do children do?. Háizimen zuò ma? 孩子们做吗？

1 AM I doing?. Wǒ zài zuò shénme?. 我在做什么？。

2 Are we doing?. Wǒmen zài zuò shénme?. 我们在做什么？。

3 Are you doing?. Nǐ zài zuò shénme?. 你在做什么？。

4 Are you doing?. Nǐ zài zuò shénme?. 你在做什么？。

5 Is he doing?. Tā zài zuò shénme?. 他在做什么？。

6 Is she doing?. Tā zài zuò shénme?. 她在做什么？。

7 Is it doing?. Shì gànma.. 是干吗。。

8 Is Ridhaan doing?. Ridhaan zài zuò shénme? Ridhaan在做什么？

9 Are they doing?. Tāmen zài zuò shénme? 他们在做什么？

10 Are children doing?. Háizimen zài zuò shénme? 孩子们在做什么？

1 Have I done?. Wǒ zuòle ma?. 我做了吗？。

2 Have we done?. Wǒmen zuò dàole ma?. 我们做到了吗？。

3 Have you done?. Nǐ gǎo hǎole méi?. 你搞好了没？。

4 Have you done?. Nǐ gǎo hǎole méi?. 你搞好了没？。

5 Has he done?. Tā zuò dàole ma?. 他做到了吗？。

6 Has she done?. Tā zuò dàole ma?. 她做到了吗？。

7 Has it done?. Zuò dàole ma?. 做到了吗？。

8 Has Ridhaan done?. Ridhaan zuòle ma? Ridhaan 做了吗？

9 Have they done?. Tāmen zuòle ma?. 他们做了吗？。
10 Have children done?. Háizimen zuòle ma? 孩子们做了吗？
1 Did I do?. Wǒ zuòle ma?. 我做了吗？。
2 Did we do?. Wǒmen zuòle ma? 我们做了吗？
3 Did you do?. Nǐ zuòle ma?. 你做了吗？。
4 Did you do?. Nǐ zuòle ma?. 你做了吗？。
5 Did he do?. Tā zuòle ma?. 他做了吗？。
6 Did she do?. Tā zuòle ma?. 她做了吗？。
7 Did it do?. Zuò dàole ma?. 做到了吗？。
8 Did Ridhaan do?. Ridhaan zuòle ma? Ridhaan 做了吗？
9 Did they do?. Tāmen zuòle ma? 他们做了吗？
10 Did children do. Háizi yǒu méiyǒu. 孩子有没有。
1 Was I doing?. Wǒ zài zuò shénme?. 我在做什么？。
2 Were we doing?. Wǒmen zài zuò shénme? 我们在做什么？
3 Were you doing?. Nǐ zài zuò shénme?. 你在做什么？。
4 Were you doing?. Nǐ zài zuò shénme?. 你在做什么？。
5 Was he doing?. Tā zài zuò shénme?. 他在做什么？。
6 Was she doing?. Tā zài zuò shénme? 她在做什么？
7 Was it doing?. Shì gàn de ma?. 是干的吗？。
8 Was Ridhaan doing?. Ridhaan zài zuò shénme? Ridhaan 在做什么？
9 Were they doing?. Tāmen zài zuò shénme? 他们在做什么？
10 Were children doing?. Háizimen zài zuò shénme? 孩子们在做什么？
1 Will I do?. Wǒ huì ma?. 我会吗？。
2 Will we do?. Wǒmen huì zuò ma? 我们会做吗？
3 Will you do?. Nǐ kěyǐ bù kěyǐ?. 你可以不可以？。
4 Will you do?. Nǐ kěyǐ bù kěyǐ?. 你可以不可以？。
5 Will he do?. Tā huì ma?. 他会吗？。
6 Will she do?. Tā huì ma?. 她会吗？。
7 Will it do?. Huì ma?. 会吗？。
8 Will Ridhaan do?. Ridhaan huì ma? Ridhaan会吗？
9 Will they do?. Tāmen huì ma?. 他们会吗？。
10 Will children do?. Háizi huì zuò ma? 孩子会做吗？
1 Will I be doing?. Wǒ huì zuò ma?. 我会做吗？。
2 Will we be doing?. Wǒmen huì zuò ma?. 我们会做吗？。
3 Will you be doing?. Nǐ huì zuò ma?. 你会做吗？。

4 Will you be doing?. Nǐ huì zuò ma?. 你会做吗？。

5 Will he be doing?. Tā huì zài zuò shénme? 他会在做什么？

6 Will she be doing?. Tā huì zài zuò shénme? 她会在做什么？

7 Will it be doing?. Huì zuò ma?. 会做吗？。

8 Will Ridhaan be doing?. Ridhaan huì zài zuò shénme? Ridhaan会在做什么？

9 Will they be doing?. Tāmen huì zuò ma?. 他们会做吗？。

10 Will children be doing?. Háizi huì zuò shénme? 孩子会做什么？

1 Will I have done?. Wǒ huì zuò ma?. 我会做吗？。

2 Will we have done?. Wǒmen huì zuò ma? 我们会做吗？

3 Will you have done?. Nǐ huì zuò ma?. 你会做吗？。

4 Will you have done?. Nǐ huì zuò ma?. 你会做吗？。

5 Will he have done?. Tā huì zuò ma? 他会做吗？

6 Will she have done?. Tā huì zuò ma? 她会做吗？

7 Will it have done?. Huì zuò ma?. 会做吗？。

8 Will Ridhaan have done?. Ridhaan huì zuò ma? Ridhaan会做吗？

9 Will they have done?. Tāmen huì zuò ma? 他们会做吗？

10 Will children have done?. Qǐngwèn háizimen zuòguò ma? 请问孩子们做过吗？

1 Can I do?. Wǒ kěbù kěyǐ zuò?. 我可不可以做？。

2 Can we do?. Wǒmen kěyǐ ma? 我们可以吗？

3 Can you do?. Nǐ kěyǐ zuò?. 你可以做？。

4 Can you do?. Nǐ kěyǐ zuò?. 你可以做？。

5 Can he do?. Tā kěyǐ ma?. 他可以吗？。

6 Can she do?. Tā kěyǐ ma?. 她可以吗？。

7 Can it do?. Kěyǐ ma?. 可以吗？。

8 Can Ridhaan do?. Ridhaan kěyǐ ma? Ridhaan可以吗？

9 Can they do?. Tāmen kěyǐ ma? 他们可以吗？

10 Can children do?. Hái zǐ kěyǐ ma? 孩子可以吗？

1 Could I do?. Wǒ kěyǐ ma?. 我可以吗？。

2 Could we do?. Wǒmen kěyǐ ma? 我们可以吗？

3 Could you do?. Nǐ néng zuò ma?. 你能做吗？。

4 Could you do?. Nǐ néng zuò ma?. 你能做吗？。

5 Could he do?. Tā kěyǐ ma?. 他可以吗？。

6 Could she do?. Tā kěyǐ ma?. 她可以吗？。

7 Could it do?. Kěyǐ ma?. 可以吗？。

8 Could Ridhaan do?. Ridhaan kěyǐ ma? Ridhaan 可以吗？

9 Could they do?. Tāmen kěyǐ ma? 他们可以吗？

10 Could children do?. Hái zǐ kěyǐ ma? 孩子可以吗？

1 Do I not do?. Wǒ bù zuò ma?. 我不做吗？。

2 Do we not do?. Wǒmen bù zuò ma?. 我们不做吗？。

3 Do you not do?. Nǐ bù zuò ma?. 你不做吗？。

4 Do you not do?. Nǐ bù zuò ma?. 你不做吗？。

5 Does he not do?. Tā bù zuò ma?. 他不做吗？。

6 Does she not do?. Tā bù zuò ma? 她不做吗？

7 Does it not do?. Bùxíng ma?. 不行吗？。

8 Does Ridhaan not do?. Ridhaan bù zuò ma? Ridhaan不做吗？

9 Do they not do?. Tāmen bù zuò ma? 他们不做吗？

10 Do children not do?. Háizi bù zuò ma? 孩子不做吗？

1 AM I not doing?. Wǒ bùshì zài zuò ma?. 我不是在做吗？。

2 Are we not doing?. Wǒmen bùshì zài zuò ma?. 我们不是在做吗？。

3 Are you not doing?. Nǐ bù gān ma?. 你不干吗？。

4 Are you not doing?. Nǐ bù gān ma?. 你不干吗？。

5 Is he not doing?. Tā bù gān ma?. 他不干吗？。

6 Is she not doing?. Tā bùshì zài zuò ma?. 她不是在做吗？。

7 Is it not doing?. Bùshì zài zuò ma?. 不是在做吗？。

8 Is Ridhaan not doing?. Ridhaan méiyǒu zài zuò ma? Ridhaan 没有在做吗？

9 Are they not doing?. Tāmen bù zuò ma?. 他们不做吗？。

10 Are children not doing?. Háizi bù gān ma? 孩子不干吗？

1 Have I not done?. Wǒ méiyǒu zuò ma?. 我没有做吗？。

2 Have we not done?. Wǒmen méiyǒu zuò ma?. 我们没有做吗？。

3 Have you not done?. Nǐ méiyǒu zuò ma?. 你没有做吗？。

4 Have you not done?. Nǐ méiyǒu zuò ma?. 你没有做吗？。

5 Has he not done?. Tā méiyǒu zuò ma?. 他没有做吗？。

6 Has she not done?. Tā méiyǒu zuò ma?. 她没有做吗？。

7 Has it not done?. Méiyǒu wánchéng ma?. 没有完成吗？。

8 Has Ridhaan not done?. Ridhaan méiyǒu zuòguò ma? Ridhaan没有做过吗？

9 Have they not done?. Tāmen méiyǒu zuò ma?. 他们没有做吗？。

10 Have children not done?. Yǒu háizi méi zuòguò ma? 有孩子没做过吗？

1 Did I not do?. Wǒ méiyǒu zuò ma?. 我没有做吗？。

2 Did we not do?. Wǒmen méiyǒu zuò ma?. 我们没有做吗？。

3 Did you not do?. Nǐ méiyǒu zuò ma?. 你没有做吗？。

4 Did you not do?. Nǐ méiyǒu zuò ma?. 你没有做吗？。

5 Did he not do?. Tā méiyǒu zuò ma?. 他没有做吗？。

6 Did she not do?. Tā méiyǒu zuò ma?. 她没有做吗？。

7 Did it not do?. Méiyǒu zuò ma?. 没有做吗？。

8 Did Ridhaan not do?. Ridhaan méiyǒu zuò ma? Ridhaan没有做吗？

9 Did they not do?. Tāmen méiyǒu zuò ma?. 他们没有做吗？。

10 Did children not do. Háizi méiyǒu zuò. 孩子没有做。

1 Was I not doing?. Wǒ bùshì zài zuò ma?. 我不是在做吗？。

2 Were we not doing?. Wǒmen bùshì zài zuò ma? 我们不是在做吗？

3 Were you not doing?. Nǐ bùshì zài zuò ma?. 你不是在做吗？。

4 Were you not doing?. Nǐ bùshì zài zuò ma?. 你不是在做吗？。

5 Was he not doing?. Tā bùshì zài zuò ma? 他不是在做吗？

6 Was she not doing?. Tā bùshì zài zuò ma? 她不是在做吗？

7 Was it not doing?. Bùshì zài zuò ma? 不是在做吗？

8 Was Ridhaan not doing?. Ridhaan méiyǒu zài zuò ma? Ridhaan 没有在做吗？

9 Were they not doing?. Tāmen bùshì zài zuò ma? 他们不是在做吗？

10 Were children not doing?. Háizimen méiyǒu zuò ma? 孩子们没有做吗？

1 Will I not do?. Wǒ bù huì ma?. 我不会吗？。

2 Will we not do?. Wǒmen bù huì ma?. 我们不会吗？。

3 Will you not do?. Nǐ bù huì ma?. 你不会吗？。

4 Will you not do?. Nǐ bù huì ma?. 你不会吗？。

5 Will he not do?. Tā bù huì ma? 他不会吗？

6 Will she not do?. Tā bù huì ma? 她不会吗？

7 Will it not do?. Bù huì ba?. 不会吧？。

8 Will Ridhaan not do?. Ridhaan bù huì ma? Ridhaan 不会吗？

9 Will they not do?. Tāmen bù huì ma? 他们不会吗？

10 Will children not do?. Háizi bù huì ma? 孩子不会吗？

1 Will I not be doing?. Wǒ bù huì zuò ma?. 我不会做吗？。

2 Will we not be doing?. Wǒmen bù huì zuò ma?. 我们不会做吗？。

3 Will you not be doing?. Nǐ bù huì zuò ma?. 你不会做吗？。

4 Will you not be doing?. Nǐ bù huì zuò ma?. 你不会做吗？。

5 Will he not be doing?. Tā bù huì zuò ma?. 他不会做吗？。

6 Will she not be doing?. Tā bù huì zuò ma? 她不会做吗？

7 Will it not be doing?. Tā bù huì zuò ma?. 它不会做吗？。

8 Will Ridhaan not be doing?. Ridhaan bù huì zuò ma? Ridhaan 不会做吗？

9 Will they not be doing?. Tāmen bù huì zuò ma? 他们不会做吗？

10 Will children not be doing?. Háizi huì bù huì zuò? 孩子会不会做？

1 Will I not have done?. Wǒ bù huì zuò ma?. 我不会做吗？。

2 Will we not have done?. Nándào wǒmen méiyǒu zuòguò ma? 难道我们没有做过吗？

3 Will you not have done?. Nǐ bù huì zuò ma?. 你不会做吗？。

4 Will you not have done?. Nǐ bù huì zuò ma?. 你不会做吗？。

5 Will he not have done?. Tā bù huì zuò ma? 他不会做吗？

6 Will she not have done?. Tā bù huì zuò ma? 她不会做吗？

7 Will it not have done?. Bù huì ba?. 不会吧？。

8 Will Ridhaan not have done?. Ridhaan bù huì zuò ma? Ridhaan 不会做吗？

9 Will they not have done?. Tāmen bù huì zuò ma? 他们不会做吗？

10 Will children not have done?. Huì bù huì háizi méi zuòguò? 会不会孩子没做过？

1 Can I not do?. Wǒ kěyǐ bù zuò ma?. 我可以不做吗？。

2 Can we not do?. Wǒmen kěyǐ bù zuò ma?. 我们可以不做吗？。

3 Can you not do?. Nǐ bùnéng ma?. 你不能吗？。

4 Can you not do?. Nǐ bùnéng ma?. 你不能吗？。

5 Can he not do?. Tā bùnéng ma?. 他不能吗？。

6 Can she not do?. Tā bùnéng ma? 她不能吗？

7 Can it not do?. Zuò bù dào ma?. 做不到吗？。

8 Can Ridhaan not do?. Ridhaan bùnéng zuò ma? Ridhaan不能做吗？

9 Can they not do?. Tāmen bùnéng ma? 他们不能吗？

10 Can children not do?. Háizi bù kěyǐ ma? 孩子不可以吗？

1 Could I not do?. Wǒ kěyǐ bù zuò ma?. 我可以不做吗？。

2 Could we not do?. Wǒmen kěyǐ bù zuò ma? 我们可以不做吗？

3 Could you not do?. Nǐ néng bù zuò ma?. 你能不做吗？。

4 Could you not do?. Nǐ néng bù zuò ma?. 你能不做吗？。

5 Could he not do?. Tā néng bù zuò ma?. 他能不做吗？。

6 Could she not do?. Tā bùnéng ma? 她不能吗？

7 Could it not do?. Kěyǐ bù zuò ma?. 可以不做吗？。

8 Could Ridhaan not do?. Ridhaan bùnéng zuò ma? Ridhaan不能做吗？

9 Could they not do?. Tāmen bùnéng zuò ma? 他们不能做吗？

10 Could children not do?. Hái zǐ néng bù zuò ma? 孩子能不做吗？

1 What do I do?. Wǒ gāi zěnme bàn?. 我该怎么办？。

2 What do we do?. Wǒmen zuò shénme?. 我们做什么？。

3 What do you do?. Nǐ zuò shénme gōngzuò?. 你做什么工作？。

4 What do you do?. Nǐ zuò shénme gōngzuò?. 你做什么工作？。

5 What does he do?. Tā zuò shénme de?. 他做什么的？。

6 What does she do?. Tā shì zuò shénme de?. 她是做什么的？。

7 What does it do?. Tā yǒu shé me zuòyòng?. 它有什么作用？。

8 What does Ridhaan do?. Ridhaan shì zuò shénme de? Ridhaan 是做什么的？

9 What do they do?. Tāmen zài zuò shénme?. 他们在做什么？。

10 What do children do?. Háizi men zuò shénme? 孩子们做什么？

1 What am I doing?. Wǒ zài zuò shénme?. 我在做什么？。

2 What are we doing?. Wǒmen zài zuò shénme?. 我们在做什么？。

3 What are you doing?. Nǐ zài gàn shénme?. 你在干什么？。

4 What are you doing?. Nǐ zài gànshénme?. 你在干什么？。

5 What is he doing?. Tā zài zuò shénme?. 他在做什么？。

6 What is she doing?. Tā zài zuò shénme?. 她在做什么？。

7 What is it doing?. Tā zài zuò shénme?. 它在做什么？。

8 What is Ridhaan doing?. Ridhaan zài zuò shénme? Ridhaan在做什么？

9 What are they doing?. Tāmen zài zuò shénme?. 他们在做什么？。

10 What are children doing?. Háizimen zài zuò shénme? 孩子们在做什么？

1 What have I done?. Wǒ zuòle shénme?. 我做了什么？。

2 What have we done?. Wǒmen zuòle shénme?. 我们做了什么？。

3 What have you done?. Nǐ zuòle shénme?. 你做了什么？。

4 What have you done?. Nǐ zuòle shénme?. 你做了什么？。

5 What has he done?. Tā zuòle shénme?. 他做了什么？。

6 What has she done?. Tā zuòle shénme?. 她做了什么？。

7 What has it done?. Tā zuòle shénme?. 它做了什么？。

8 What has Ridhaan done?. Ridhaan zuòle shénme? Ridhaan 做了什么？

9 What have they done?. Tāmen zuòle shénme?. 他们做了什么？。

10 What have children done?. Háizimen zuòle shénme? 孩子们做了什么？

1 What did I do?. Wǒ zuòle shénme?. 我做了什么？。

2 What did we do?. Wǒmen zuòle shénme?. 我们做了什么？。

3 What did you do?. Nǐ zuòle shénme?. 你做了什么？。

4 What did you do?. Nǐ zuòle shénme?. 你做了什么？。

5 What did he do?. Tā zuòle shénme?. 他做了什么？。

6 What did she do?. Tā zuòle shénme?. 她做了什么？。

7 What did it do?. Tā zuòle shénme?. 它做了什么？。

8 What did Ridhaan do?. Ridhaan zuòle shénme? Ridhaan 做了什么？

9 What did they do?. Tāmen zuòle shénme?. 他们做了什么？。

10 What did children do. Háizimen zuòle shénme. 孩子们做了什么。

1 What was I doing?. Wǒ zài zuò shénme?. 我在做什么？。

2 What were we doing?. Wǒmen zài zuò shénme? 我们在做什么？

3 What were you doing?. Nǐ zài zuò shénme?. 你在做什么？。

4 What were you doing?. Nǐ zài zuò shénme?. 你在做什么？。

5 What was he doing?. Tā zài zuò shénme?. 他在做什么？。

6 What was she doing?. Tā zài zuò shénme?. 她在做什么？。

7 What was it doing?. Tā zài zuò shénme?. 它在做什么？。

8 What was Ridhaan doing?. Ridhaan zài zuò shénme? Ridhaan 在做什么？

9 What were they doing?. Tāmen zài gànshénme?. 他们在干什么？。

10 What were children doing?. Háizimen zài zuò shénme? 孩子们在做什么？

1 What will I do?. Wǒ gāi zěnme bàn?. 我该怎么办？。

2 What will we do?. Wǒmen huì zěnyàng zuò?. 我们会怎样做？。

3 What will you do?. Nǐ huì zěnme zuò?. 你会怎么做？。

4 What will you do?. Nǐ huì zěnme zuò?. 你会怎么做？。

5 What will he do?. Tā huì zěnme zuò?. 他会怎么做？。

6 What will she do?. Tā huì zěnme zuò?. 她会怎么做？。

7 What will it do?. Tā huì zuò shénme?. 它会做什么？。

8 What will Ridhaan do?. Ridhaan huì zuò shénme? Ridhaan 会做什么？

9 What will they do?. Tāmen huì zěnme zuò?. 他们会怎么做？。

10 What will children do?. Háizimen huì zěnme zuò?. 孩子们会怎么做？。

1 What will I be doing?. Wǒ yào zuò shénme?. 我要做什么？。

2 What will we be doing?. Wǒmen jiāng zuò shénme?. 我们将做什么？。

3 What will you be doing?. Nǐ huì zuò shénme?. 你会做什么？。

4 What will you be doing?. Nǐ huì zuò shénme?. 你会做什么？。

5 What will he be doing?. Tā huì zuò shénme?. 他会做什么？。

6 What will she be doing?. Tā huì zuò shénme?. 她会做什么？。

7 What will it be doing?. Tā huì zuò shénme?. 它会做什么？。

8 What will Ridhaan be doing?. Ridhaan huì zuò shénme? Ridhaan 会做什么？

9 What will they be doing?. Tāmen huì zuò shénme?. 他们会做什么？。

10 What will children be doing?. Háizimen huì zuò shénme? 孩子们会做什么？

1 What will I have done?. Wǒ huì zěnme zuò?. 我会怎么做？。

2 What will we have done?. Wǒmen huì zuò shénme? 我们会做什么？

3 What will you have done?. Nǐ huì zěnme zuò?. 你会怎么做？。

4 What will you have done?. Nǐ huì zěnme zuò?. 你会怎么做？。

5 What will he have done?. Tā huì zěnme zuò? 他会怎么做？

6 What will she have done?. Tā huì zěnme zuò? 她会怎么做？

7 What will it have done?. Tā huì zuò shénme?. 它会做什么？。

8 What will Ridhaan have done?. Ridhaan huì zuò shénme? Ridhaan 会做什么？

9 What will they have done?. Tāmen huì zěnme zuò? 他们会怎么做？

10 What will children have done?. Háizimen huì zuò shénme? 孩子们会做什么？

1 What can I do?. Wǒ néng zuò shénme?. 我能做什么？。

2 What can we do?. Wǒmen néng zuò shénme?. 我们能做什么？。

3 What can you do?. Nǐ néng zuò shénme?. 你能做什么？。

4 What can you do?. Nǐ néng zuò shénme?. 你能做什么？。

5 What can he do?. Tā néng zuò shénme?. 他能做什么？。

6 What can she do?. Tā néng zuò shénme?. 她能做什么？。

7 What can it do?. Tā néng zuò shénme?. 它能做什么？。

8 What can Ridhaan do?. Ridhaan néng zuò shénme? Ridhaan 能做什么？

9 What can they do?. Tāmen néng zuò shénme?. 他们能做什么？。

10 What can children do?. Hái zǐ néng zuò shénme? 孩子能做什么？

1 What could I do?. Wǒ néng zuò shénme?. 我能做什么？。

2 What could we do?. Wǒmen néng zuò shénme? 我们能做什么？

3 What could you do?. Nǐ néng zuò shénme? 你能做什么？

4 What could you do?. Nǐ néng zuò shénme? 你能做什么？

5 What could he do?. Tā néng zuò shénme? 他能做什么？

6 What could she do?. Tā néng zuò shénme? 她能做什么？

7 What could it do?. Tā néng zuò shénme? 它能做什么？

8 What could Ridhaan do?. Ridhaan néng zuò shénme? Ridhaan 能做什么？

9 What could they do?. Tāmen néng zuò shénme? 他们能做什么？

10 What could children do?. Hái zǐ néng zuò shénme? 孩子能做什么？

1 What do I not do?. Wǒ bù zuò shénme? 我不做什么？

2 What do we not do?. Wǒmen bù zuò shénme? 我们不做什么？

3 What do you not do?. Nǐ bù zuò shénme?. 你不做什么？。

4 What do you not do?. Nǐ bù zuò shénme?. 你不做什么？。

5 What does he not do?. Tā bù zuò shénme? 他不做什么？

6 What does she not do?. Tā bù zuò shénme? 她不做什么？

7 What does it not do?. Tā bù zuò shénme?. 它不做什么？。

8 What does Ridhaan not do?. Ridhaan bù zuò shénme? Ridhaan 不做什么？

9 What do they not do?. Tāmen bù zuò shénme? 他们不做什么？

10 What do children not do?. Háizi bù zuò shénme? 孩子不做什么？

1 What am I not doing?. Wǒ bù zuò shénme?. 我不做什么？。

2 What are we not doing?. Wǒmen bù zuò shénme?. 我们不做什么？。

3 What are you not doing?. Nǐ bù zuò shénme?. 你不做什么？。

4 What are you not doing?. Nǐ bù zuò shénme?. 你不做什么？。

5 What is he not doing?. Tā bù zuò shénme?. 他不做什么？。

6 What is she not doing?. Tā bù zuò shénme?. 她不做什么？。

7 What is it not doing?. Tā bù zuò shénme?. 它不做什么？。

8 What is Ridhaan not doing?. Ridhaan méiyǒu zuò shénme? Ridhaan 没有做什么？

9 What are they not doing?. Tāmen bù zuò shénme?. 他们不做什么？。

10 What are children not doing?. Háizi bù zuò shénme? 孩子不做什么？

1 What have I not done?. Wǒ hái méiyǒu zuò shénme?. 我还没有做什么？。

2 What have we not done?. Wǒmen hái méiyǒu zuò shénme?. 我们还没有做什么？。

3 What have you not done?. Nǐ yǒu shé me méiyǒu zuò?. 你有什么没有做？。

4 What have you not done?. Nǐ yǒu shé me méiyǒu zuò?. 你有什么没有做？。

5 What has he not done?. Tā yǒu shé me méiyǒu zuò? 他有什么没有做？

6 What has she not done?. Tā yǒu shé me méiyǒu zuò? 她有什么没有做？

7 What has it not done?. Tā méiyǒu zuò shénme?. 它没有做什么？。

8 What has Ridhaan not done?. Ridhaan méiyǒu zuò shénme? Ridhaan 没有做什么？

9 What have they not done?. Tāmen méiyǒu zuò shénme?. 他们没有做什么？。

10 What have children not done?. Háizi men méiyǒu zuòguò shèn me? 孩子们没有做过什么？

1 What did I not do?. Wǒ méiyǒu zuò shénme?. 我没有做什么？。

2 What did we not do?. Wǒmen méiyǒu zuò shénme?. 我们没有做什么？。

3 What did you not do?. Nǐ méiyǒu zuò shénme?. 你没有做什么？。

4 What did you not do?. Nǐ méiyǒu zuò shénme?. 你没有做什么？。

5 What did he not do?. Tā méiyǒu zuò shénme?. 他没有做什么？。

6 What did she not do?. Tā méiyǒu zuò shénme?. 她没有做什么？。

7 What did it not do?. Tā méiyǒu zuò shénme?. 它没有做什么？。

8 What did Ridhaan not do?. Ridhaan méiyǒu zuò shénme? Ridhaan 没有做什么？

9 What did they not do?. Tāmen méiyǒu zuò shénme?. 他们没有做什么？。

10 What did children not do. Háizi men méiyǒu zuò shénme. 孩子们没有做什么。

1 What was I not doing?. Wǒ méiyǒu zuò shénme?. 我没有做什么？。

2 What were we not doing?. Wǒmen méiyǒu zuò shénme?. 我们没有做什么？。

3 What were you not doing?. Nǐ méiyǒu zuò shénme?. 你没有做什么？。

4 What were you not doing?. Nǐ méiyǒu zuò shénme?. 你没有做什么？。

5 What was he not doing?. Tā méiyǒu zuò shénme?. 他没有做什么？。

6 What was she not doing?. Tā méiyǒu zuò shénme?. 她没有做什么？。

7 What was it not doing?. Tā méiyǒu zuò shénme?. 它没有做什么？。

8 What was Ridhaan not doing?. Ridhaan méiyǒu zuò shénme? Ridhaan 没有做什么？

9 What were they not doing?. Tāmen méiyǒu zuò shénme?. 他们没有做什么？。

10 What were children not doing?. Háizimen méiyǒu zuò shénme? 孩子们没有做什么？

1 What will I not do?. Wǒ bù huì zuò shénme?. 我不会做什么？。

2 What will we not do?. Wǒmen bù huì zuò shénme? 我们不会做什么？

3 What will you not do?. Nǐ bù huì zuò shénme?. 你不会做什么？。

4 What will you not do?. Nǐ bù huì zuò shénme?. 你不会做什么？。

5 What will he not do?. Tā bù huì zuò shénme? 他不会做什么？

6 What will she not do?. Tā bù huì zuò shénme? 她不会做什么？

7 What will it not do?. Tā bù huì zuò shénme?. 它不会做什么？。

8 What will Ridhaan not do?. Ridhaan bù huì zuò shénme? Ridhaan 不会做什么？

9 What will they not do?. Tāmen bù huì zuò shénme? 他们不会做什么？

10 What will children not do?. Háizi bù huì zuò shénme? 孩子不会做什么？

1 What will I not be doing?. Wǒ bù huì zuò shénme?. 我不会做什么？。

2 What will we not be doing?. Wǒmen bù huì zuò shénme? 我们不会做什么？

3 What will you not be doing?. Nǐ bù huì zuò shénme? 你不会做什么？

4 What will you not be doing?. Nǐ bù huì zuò shénme? 你不会做什么？

5 What will he not be doing?. Tā bù huì zuò shénme? 他不会做什么？

6 What will she not be doing?. Tā bù huì zuò shénme? 她不会做什么？

7 What will it not be doing?. Tā bù huì zuò shénme?. 它不会做什么？。

8 What will Ridhaan not be doing?. Ridhaan bù huì zuò shénme? Ridhaan 不会做什么？

9 What will they not be doing?. Tāmen bù huì zuò shénme? 他们不会做什么？

10 What will children not be doing?. Háizi bù huì zuò shénme? 孩子不会做什么？

1 What will I not have done?. Shénme shì wǒ méiyǒu zuò de? 什么是我没有做的？

2 What will we not have done?. Shénme shì wǒmen méiyǒu zuò de? 什么是我们没有做的？

3 What will you not have done?. Nǐ bù huì zuò shénme? 你不会做什么？

4 What will you not have done?. Nǐ bù huì zuò shénme? 你不会做什么？

5 What will he not have done?. Tā bù huì zuò shénme? 他不会做什么？

6 What will she not have done?. Tā bù huì zuò shénme? 她不会做什么？

7 What will it not have done?. Tā bù huì zuò shénme? 它不会做什么？

8 What will Ridhaan not have done?. Ridhaan huì zuò shénme? Ridhaan 会做什么？

9 What will they not have done?. Tāmen bù huì zuò shénme? 他们不会做什么？

10 What will children not have done?. Háizimen bù huì zuò shénme? 孩子们不会做什么？

1 What can I not do?. Wǒ bùnéng zuò shénme?. 我不能做什么？。

2 What can we not do?. Wǒmen bùnéng zuò shénme? 我们不能做什么？

3 What can you not do?. Nǐ bùnéng zuò shénme?. 你不能做什么？。

4 What can you not do?. Nǐ bùnéng zuò shénme?. 你不能做什么？。

5 What can he not do?. Tā yǒu shé me bùnéng zuò de? 他有什么不能做的？

6 What can she not do?. Tā yǒu shé me bùnéng zuò de? 她有什么不能做的？

7 What can it not do?. Shénme bùnéng zuò?. 什么不能做？。

8 What can Ridhaan not do?. Ridhaan bùnéng zuò shénme? Ridhaan 不能做什么？

9 What can they not do?. Tāmen bùnéng zuò shénme?. 他们不能做什么？。

10 What can children not do?. Háizi bùnéng zuò shénme? 孩子不能做什么？

1 What could I not do?. Wǒ bùnéng zuò shénme? 我不能做什么？

2 What could we not do?. Wǒmen bùnéng zuò shénme? 我们不能做什么？

3 What could you not do?. Nǐ bùnéng zuò shénme? 你不能做什么？

4 What could you not do?. Nǐ bùnéng zuò shénme? 你不能做什么？

5 What could he not do?. Tā yǒu shé me bùnéng zuò de? 他有什么不能做的？

6 What could she not do?. Tā yǒu shé me bùnéng zuò de? 她有什么不能做的？

7 What could it not do?. Tā bùnéng zuò shénme?. 它不能做什么？。

8 What could Ridhaan not do?. Ridhaan yǒu shé me bùnéng zuò de? Ridhaan 有什么不能做的？

9 What could they not do?. Tāmen bùnéng zuò shénme? 他们不能做什么？

10 What could children not do?. Háizi yǒu shé me bùnéng zuò de? 孩子有什么不能做的？

Chapter 2 Dì 2 zhāng 第2章

1 Go verb Qù dòngcí 去动词

2 I go. wǒ qù. 我去。

3 I am going. Wǒ yào qù. 我要去。

4 I have gone. Wǒ zǒule. 我走了。

5 I went. Wǒ qùle. 我去了。

6 I was going. Wǒ zhèng xiǎng. 我正想。

7 I will go. Wǒ yào zǒule. 我要走了。

8 I will be going. Wǒ jiāngyào qù. 我将要去。

9 I will have gone. Wǒ huì zǒule. 我会走了。

10 I can go. Wǒ kěyǐ qù. 我可以去。

I could go. Wǒ kěyǐ qù. 我可以去。

Write verb Xiě dòngcí 写动词

1 I write. wǒ xiě de. 我写的。

2 I am writing. Wǒ zài xiě xìn. 我在写信。

3 I have written. Wǒ yǐjīng xiěle. 我已经写了。

4 I wrote. Wǒ xiě. 我写。

5 I was writing. Wǒ zhèngzài xiězuò. 我正在写作。

6 I will write. Wǒ huì xiě. 我会写。

7 I will be writing. Wǒ huì xiě de. 我会写的。

8 I will have written. Wǒ huì xiě de. 我会写的。

9 I can write. Wǒ kěyǐ xiě. 我可以写。

10 I could write. Wǒ kěyǐ xiě. 我可以写。

1 I go. Wǒ qù. 我去。

2 We go. Wǒmen qù. 我们去。

3 You go. Nǐ zǒu. 你走。

4 You go. Nǐ zǒu. 你走。

5 He goes. Tā qù. 他去。

6 She goes. Tā qù. 她去。

7 It goes. Tā qù. 它去。

8 Ridhaan goes. Lǐ dān qù. 里丹去。

9 They go. Tāmen qù. 他们去。

10 Children go. Háizimen qù. 孩子们去。

1 I write. Wǒ xiě de. 我写的。

2 We write. Wǒmen xiě. 我们写。

3 You write. Nǐ xiě. 你写。

4 You write. Nǐ xiě. 你写。

5 He writes. Tā xiě. 他写。

6 She writes. Tā xiě. 她写。

7 It writes. Tā xiě dào. 它写道。

8 Ridhaan writes. Lǐ dān xiě dào. 里丹写道。

9 They write. Tāmen xiě. 他们写。

10 Children write. Háizimen xiě. 孩子们写。

1 I am going. Wǒ yào qù. 我要去。

2 We are going. Wǒmen yào zǒule. 我们要走了。

3 You are going. Nǐ yào qù. 你要去。

4 You are going. Nǐ yào qù. 你要去。

5 He is going. Tā yào qù. 他要去。

6 She is going. Tā yào qù. 她要去。

7 It is going. Tā jiāngyào. 它将要。

8 Ridhaan is going. Lǐ dān yào zǒule. 里丹要走了。

9 They are going. Tāmen jiāng. 他们将。

10 Children are going. Háizimen yào qù. 孩子们要去。

1 I am writing. Wǒ zài xiě xìn. 我在写信。

2 We are writing. Wǒmen zhèngzài xiězuò. 我们正在写作。

3 You are writing. Nǐ zài xiězuò. 你在写作。

4 You are writing. Nǐ zài xiězuò. 你在写作。

5 He is writing. Tā zài xiězuò. 他在写作。
6 She is writing. Tā zài xiězuò. 她在写作。
7 It is writing. Tā zhèngzài xiězuò. 它正在写作。
8 Ridhaan is writing. Lǐ dān zhèngzài xiězuò. 里丹正在写作。
9 They are writing. Tāmen zài xiězuò. 他们在写作。
10 Children are writing. Háizimen zhèngzài xiězuò. 孩子们正在写作。
1 I have gone. Wǒ zǒule. 我走了。
2 We have gone. Wǒmen yǐjīng zǒule. 我们已经走了。
3 You have gone. Nǐ yǐjīng zǒule. 你已经走了。
4 You have gone. Nǐ yǐjīng zǒule. 你已经走了。
5 He has gone. Tā zǒule. 他走了。
6 She has gone. Tā zǒule. 她走了。
7 It has gone. Tā yǐjīng guòqùle. 它已经过去了。
8 Ridhaan has gone. Ruì dān zǒule. 瑞丹走了。
9 They have gone. Tāmen zǒule. 他们走了。
10 Children have gone. Háizimen zǒule. 孩子们走了。
1 I have written. Wǒ yǐjīng xiěle. 我已经写了。
2 We have written. Wǒmen yǐjīng xiěle. 我们已经写了。
3 You have written. Nǐ xiě. 你写。
4 You have written. Nǐ xiě. 你写。
5 He has written. Tā xiěguò. 他写过。
6 She has written. Tā xiěguò. 她写过。
7 It has written. Tā xiěle. 它写了。
8 Ridhaan has written. Ridhaan yǐjīng xiěle. Ridhaan 已经写了。
9 They have written. Tāmen xiěle. 他们写了。
10 Children have written. Háizimen xiěle. 孩子们写了。
1 I went. Wǒ qùle. 我去了。
2 We went. Wǒmen qùle. 我们去了。
3 You went. Nǐ qùle. 你去了。
4 You went. Nǐ qùle. 你去了。
5 He went. Tā qù. 他去。
6 She went. Tā qù. 她去。
7 It went. Tā qù. 它去。
8 Ridhaan went. Lǐ dān qùle. 里丹去了。
9 They went. Tāmen qùle. 他们去了。
10 Children went. Háizimen qùle. 孩子们去了。

1 I wrote. Wǒ xiě. 我写。

2 We wrote. Wǒmen xiě. 我们写。

3 You wrote. Nǐ xiěle. 你写了。

4 You wrote. Nǐ xiěle. 你写了。

5 He wrote. Tā xiěle. 他写了。

6 She wrote. Tā xiěle. 她写了。

7 It wrote. Tā xiě dào. 它写道。

8 Ridhaan wrote. Lǐ dān xiě dào. 里丹写道。

9 They wrote. Tāmen xiě. 他们写。

10 Children wrote. Háizimen xiěle. 孩子们写了。

1 I was going. Wǒ zhèng xiǎng. 我正想。

2 We were going. Wǒmen yào qù. 我们要去。

3 You were going. Nǐ yào qù. 你要去。

4 You were going. Nǐ yào qù. 你要去。

5 He was going. Tā yào qù. 他要去。

6 She was going. Tā yào qù. 她要去。

7 It was going. Tā zhèngzài qù. 它正在去。

8 Ridhaan was going. Ridhaan yào qù. Ridhaan要去。

9 They were going. Tāmen yào qù. 他们要去。

10 Children were going. Háizimen qù. 孩子们去。

1 I was writing. Wǒ zhèngzài xiězuò. 我正在写作。

2 We were writing. Wǒmen zhèngzài xiězuò. 我们正在写作。

3 You were writing. Nǐ zài xiězuò. 你在写作。

4 You were writing. Nǐ zài xiězuò. 你在写作。

5 He was writing. Tā zhèngzài xiězuò. 他正在写作。

6 She was writing. Tā zài xiězuò. 她在写作。

7 It was writing. Tā zhèngzài xiězuò. 它正在写作。

8 Ridhaan was writing. Lǐ dān zhèngzài xiězuò. 里丹正在写作。

9 They were writing. Tāmen zhèngzài xiězuò. 他们正在写作。

10 Children were writing. Háizimen zhèngzài xiězuò. 孩子们正在写作。

1 I will go. Wǒ yào zǒule. 我要走了。

2 We will go. Wǒmen huì qù. 我们会去。

3 You will go. Nǐ jiāng qù. 你将去。

4 You will go. Nǐ jiāng qù. 你将去。

5 He will go. Tā huì qù. 他会去。

6 She will go. Tā huì qù. 她会去。

7 It will go. Tā huì qù. 它会去。

8 Ridhaan will go. Lǐ dān huì qù. 里丹会去。

9 They will go. Tāmen huì qù. 他们会去。

10 Children will go. Háizimen huì qù. 孩子们会去。

1 I will write. Wǒ huì xiě. 我会写。

2 We will write. Wǒmen huì xiě. 我们会写。

3 You will write. Nǐ huì xiě. 你会写。

4 You will write. Nǐ huì xiě. 你会写。

5 He will write. Tā huì xiě. 他会写。

6 She will write. Tā huì xiě. 她会写。

7 It will write. Tā huì xiě. 它会写。

8 Ridhaan will write. Ridhaan huì xiě. Ridhaan 会写。

9 They will write. Tāmen huì xiě. 他们会写。

10 Children will write. Háizimen huì xiě. 孩子们会写。

1 I will be going. Wǒ jiāngyào qù. 我将要去。

2 We will be going. Wǒmen huì qù de. 我们会去的。

3 You will be going. Nǐ huì qù de. 你会去的。

4 You will be going. Nǐ huì qù de. 你会去的。

5 He will be going. Tā huì qù de. 他会去的。

6 She will be going. Tā huì qù de. 她会去的。

7 It will be going. Tā huì qù de. 它会去的。

8 Ridhaan will be going. Ridhaan huì qù de. Ridhaan会去的。

9 They will be going. Tāmen huì qù de. 他们会去的。

10 Children will be going. Háizimen huì qù de. 孩子们会去的。

1 I will be writing. Wǒ huì xiě de. 我会写的。

2 We will be writing. Wǒmen jiāng xiězuò. 我们将写作。

3 You will be writing. Nǐ huì xiězuò. 你会写作。

4 You will be writing. Nǐ huì xiězuò. 你会写作。

5 He will be writing. Tā huì xiězuò. 他会写作。

6 She will be writing. Tā huì xiězuò. 她会写作。

7 It will be writing. Huì xiě de. 会写的。

8 Ridhaan will be writing. Ridhaan jiāng xiězuò. Ridhaan 将写作。

9 They will be writing. Tāmen huì xiězuò. 他们会写作。

10 Children will be writing. Háizimen huì xiě. 孩子们会写。

1 I will have gone. Wǒ huì zǒule. 我会走了。

2 We will have gone. Wǒmen huì zǒule. 我们会走了。

3 You will have gone. Nǐ huì zǒule. 你会走了。

4 You will have gone. Nǐ huì zǒule. 你会走了。

5 He will have gone. Tā huì zǒule. 他会走了。

6 She will have gone. Tā huì zǒule. 她会走了。

7 It will have gone. Tā huì guòqù de. 它会过去的。

8 Ridhaan will have gone. Ridhaan huì líkāi de. Ridhaan 会离开的。

9 They will have gone. Tāmen huì zǒule. 他们会走了。

10 Children will have gone. Háizimen dūhuì zǒule. 孩子们都会走了。

1 I will have written. Wǒ huì xiě de. 我会写的。

2 We will have written. Wǒmen huì xiě de. 我们会写的。

3 You will have written. Nǐ huì xiě de. 你会写的。

4 You will have written. Nǐ huì xiě de. 你会写的。

5 He will have written. Tā huì xiě de. 他会写的。

6 She will have written. Tā huì xiě de. 她会写的。

7 It will have written. Tā huì xiě. 它会写。

8 Ridhaan will have written. Ridhaan huì xiě de. Ridhaan 会写的。

9 They will have written. Tāmen huì xiě de. 他们会写的。

10 Children will have written. Háizimen huì xiě de. 孩子们会写的。

1 I can go. Wǒ kěyǐ qù. 我可以去。

2 We can go. Wǒmen kěyǐ qù. 我们可以去。

3 You can go. Nǐ kěyǐ zǒule. 你可以走了。

4 You can go. Nǐ kěyǐ zǒule. 你可以走了。

5 He can go. Tā kěyǐ qù. 他可以去。

6 She can go. Tā kěyǐ zǒule. 她可以走了。

7 It can go. Tā kěyǐ qù. 它可以去。

8 Ridhaan can go. Ridhaan kěyǐ qù. Ridhaan可以去。

9 They can go. Tāmen kěyǐ qù. 他们可以去。

10 Children can go. Háizimen kěyǐ qù. 孩子们可以去。

1 I can write. Wǒ kěyǐ xiě. 我可以写。

2 We can write. Wǒmen kěyǐ xiě. 我们可以写。

3 You can write. Nǐ kěyǐ xiě. 你可以写。

4 You can write. Nǐ kěyǐ xiě. 你可以写。

5 He can write. Tā kěyǐ xiě. 他可以写。

6 She can write. Tā huì xiě. 她会写。

7 It can write. Tā kěyǐ xiě. 它可以写。

8 Ridhaan can write. Ridhaan kěyǐ xiě. Ridhaan 可以写。

9 They can write. Tāmen kěyǐ xiě. 他们可以写。

10 Children can write. Háizimen kěyǐ xiě. 孩子们可以写。

1 I could go. Wǒ kěyǐ qù. 我可以去。

2 We could go. Wǒmen kěyǐ qù. 我们可以去。

3 You could go. Nǐ kěyǐ qù. 你可以去。

4 You could go. Nǐ kěyǐ qù. 你可以去。

5 He could go. Tā kěyǐ qù. 他可以去。

6 She could go. Tā kěyǐ zǒule. 她可以走了。

7 It could go. Tā kěyǐ qù. 它可以去。

8 Ridhaan could go. Ridhaan kěyǐ qù. Ridhaan可以去。

9 They could go. Tāmen kěyǐ qù. 他们可以去。

10 Children could go. Háizimen kěyǐ qù. 孩子们可以去。

1 I could write. Wǒ kěyǐ xiě. 我可以写。

2 We could write. Wǒmen kěyǐ xiě. 我们可以写。

3 You could write. Nǐ kěyǐ xiě. 你可以写。

4 You could write. Nǐ kěyǐ xiě. 你可以写。

5 He could write. Tā kěyǐ xiě. 他可以写。

6 She could write. Tā kěyǐ xiě. 她可以写。

7 It could write. Tā kěyǐ xiě. 它可以写。

8 Ridhaan could write. Ridhaan kěyǐ xiě. Ridhaan 可以写。

9 They could write. Tāmen kěyǐ xiě. 他们可以写。

10 Children could write. Háizimen kěyǐ xiě. 孩子们可以写。

1 I do not go. Wǒ bù qù. 我不去。

2 We do not go. Wǒmen bù qù. 我们不去。

3 You do not go. Nǐ bù qù. 你不去。

4 You do not go. Nǐ bù qù. 你不去。

5 He does not go. Tā bù qù. 他不去。

6 She does not go. Tā bù qù. 她不去。

7 It does not go. Tā bù qù. 它不去。

8 Ridhaan does not go. Ridhaan méiyǒu qù. Ridhaan没有去。

9 They do not go. Tāmen bù qù. 他们不去。

10 Children do not go. Háizi bù qù. 孩子不去。

1 I do not write. Wǒ bù xiě. 我不写。

2 We do not write. Wǒmen bù xiě. 我们不写。

3 You do not write. Nǐ bù xiě. 你不写。

4 You do not write. Nǐ bù xiě. 你不写。

5 He does not write. Tā bù xiě. 他不写。

6 She does not write. Tā bù xiě. 她不写。

7 It does not write. Tā bù xiě. 它不写。

8 Ridhaan does not write. Ridhaan bù xiě. Ridhaan 不写。

9 They do not write. Tāmen bù xiě. 他们不写。

10 Children do not write. Háizi bù xiě. 孩子不写。

1 I am not going. Wǒ bù dǎsuàn. 我不打算。

2 We are not going. Wǒmen bù qù. 我们不去。

3 You are not going. Nǐ bù qù. 你不去。

4 You are not going. Nǐ bù qù. 你不去。

5 He is not going. Tā bù qù. 他不去。

6 She is not going. Tā bù qù. 她不去。

7 It is not going. Tā bù huì qù. 它不会去。

8 Ridhaan is not going. Ridhaan bù qù. Ridhaan 不去。

9 They are not going. Tāmen bù qù. 他们不去。

10 Children are not going. Háizimen bù qù. 孩子们不去。

1 I am not writing. Wǒ bùshì zài xiě. 我不是在写。

2 We are not writing. Wǒmen bùshì zài xiězuò. 我们不是在写作。

3 You are not writing. Nǐ bùshì zài xiě. 你不是在写。

4 You are not writing. Nǐ bùshì zài xiě. 你不是在写。

5 He is not writing. Tā bùshì zài xiězuò. 他不是在写作。

6 She is not writing. Tā bùshì zài xiězuò. 她不是在写作。

7 It is not writing. Zhè bùshì xiězuò. 这不是写作。

8 Ridhaan is not writing. Ridhaan méiyǒu zài xiězuò. Ridhaan 没有在写作。

9 They are not writing. Tāmen bùshì zài xiězuò. 他们不是在写作。

10 Children are not writing. Háizi bù xiě. 孩子不写。

1 I have not gone. Wǒ méiyǒu qù. 我没有去。

2 We have not gone. Wǒmen méiyǒu qù. 我们没有去。

3 You have not gone. Nǐ hái méi zǒu. 你还没走。

4 You have not gone. Nǐ hái méi zǒu. 你还没走。

5 He has not gone. Tā hái méiyǒu zǒu. 他还没有走。

6 She has not gone. Tā hái méiyǒu zǒu. 她还没有走。

7 It has not gone. Tā méiyǒu xiāoshī. 它没有消失。

8 Ridhaan has not gone. Ridhaan méiyǒu zǒu. Ridhaan没有走。

9 They have not gone. Tāmen hái méiyǒu zǒu. 他们还没有走。

10 Children have not gone. Háizimen méiyǒu zǒu. 孩子们没有走。

1 I have not written. Wǒ méiyǒu xiě. 我没有写。

2 We have not written. Wǒmen hái méiyǒu xiě. 我们还没有写。

3 You have not written. Nǐ hái méiyǒu xiě. 你还没有写。

4 You have not written. Nǐ hái méiyǒu xiě. 你还没有写。

5 He has not written. Tā méiyǒu xiě. 他没有写。

6 She has not written. Tā méiyǒu xiě. 她没有写。

7 It has not written. Tā méiyǒu xiě. 它没有写。

8 Ridhaan has not written. Ridhaan méiyǒu xiě. Ridhaan 没有写。

9 They have not written. Tāmen méiyǒu xiě. 他们没有写。

10 Children have not written. Háizi méiyǒu xiě. 孩子没有写。

1 I did not go. Wǒ méiyǒu qù. 我没有去。

2 We did not go. Wǒmen méiyǒu qù. 我们没有去。

3 You did not go. Nǐ méiyǒu qù. 你没有去。

4 You did not go. Nǐ méiyǒu qù. 你没有去。

5 He did not go. Tā méiyǒu qù. 他没有去。

6 She did not go. Tā méiyǒu qù. 她没有去。

7 It did not go. Tā méiyǒu qù. 它没有去。

8 Ridhaan did not go. Ridhaan méiyǒu qù. Ridhaan没有去。

9 They did not go. Tāmen méiyǒu qù. 他们没有去。

10 Children did not go. Háizimen méiyǒu qù. 孩子们没有去。

1 I did not write. Wǒ méiyǒu xiě. 我没有写。

2 We did not write. Wǒmen méiyǒu xiě. 我们没有写。

3 You did not write. Nǐ méiyǒu xiě. 你没有写。

4 You did not write. Nǐ méiyǒu xiě. 你没有写。

5 He did not write. Tā méiyǒu xiě. 他没有写。

6 She did not write. Tā méiyǒu xiě. 她没有写。

7 It did not write. Tā méiyǒu xiě. 它没有写。

8 Ridhaan did not write. Ridhaan méiyǒu xiě. Ridhaan 没有写。

9 They did not write. Tāmen méiyǒu xiě. 他们没有写。

10 Children did not write. Háizi méiyǒu xiě. 孩子没有写。

1 I was not going. Wǒ méiyǒu qù. 我没有去。

2 We were not going. Wǒmen méiyǒu qù. 我们没有去。

3 You were not going. Nǐ méiyǒu qù. 你没有去。

4 You were not going. Nǐ méiyǒu qù. 你没有去。

5 He was not going. Tā bù qù. 他不去。

6 She was not going. Tā bù qù. 她不去。

7 It was not going. Tā méiyǒu qù. 它没有去。

8 Ridhaan was not going. Ridhaan méiyǒu qù. Ridhaan没有去。

9 They were not going. Tāmen bù qù. 他们不去。

10 Children were not going. Háizimen bù qù. 孩子们不去。

1 I was not writing. Wǒ bùshì zài xiě. 我不是在写。

2 We were not writing. Wǒmen bùshì zài xiězuò. 我们不是在写作。

3 You were not writing. Nǐ bùshì zài xiě. 你不是在写。

4 You were not writing. Nǐ bùshì zài xiě. 你不是在写。

5 He was not writing. Tā bùshì zài xiězuò. 他不是在写作。

6 She was not writing. Tā bùshì zài xiězuò. 她不是在写作。

7 It was not writing. Zhè bùshì xiězuò. 这不是写作。

8 Ridhaan was not writing. Ridhaan méiyǒu zài xiězuò. Ridhaan 没有在写作。

9 They were not writing. Tāmen bùshì zài xiězuò. 他们不是在写作。

10 Children were not writing. Háizimen méiyǒu xiě. 孩子们没有写。

1 I will not go. Wǒ bù huì qù. 我不会去。

2 We will not go. Wǒmen bù huì qù. 我们不会去。

3 You will not go. Nǐ bù huì qù de. 你不会去的。

4 You will not go. Nǐ bù huì qù de. 你不会去的。

5 He will not go. Tā bù huì qù. 他不会去。

6 She will not go. Tā bù huì qù. 她不会去。

7 It will not go. Tā bù huì qù. 它不会去。

8 Ridhaan will not go. Ridhaan bù huì qù. Ridhaan不会去。

9 They will not go. Tāmen bù huì qù. 他们不会去。

10 Children will not go. Háizi bù huì qù. 孩子不会去。

1 I will not write. Wǒ bù huì xiě. 我不会写。

2 We will not write. Wǒmen bù huì xiě. 我们不会写。

3 You will not write. Nǐ bù huì xiě. 你不会写。

4 You will not write. Nǐ bù huì xiě. 你不会写。

5 He will not write. Tā bù huì xiě. 他不会写。

6 She will not write. Tā bù huì xiě. 她不会写。

7 It will not write. Tā bù huì xiě. 它不会写。

8 Ridhaan will not write. Ridhaan bù huì xiě. Ridhaan 不会写。

9 They will not write. Tāmen bù huì xiě. 他们不会写。

10 Children will not write. Háizi bù huì xiě. 孩子不会写。

1 I will not be going. Wǒ bù huì qù de. 我不会去的。

2 We will not be going. Wǒmen bù huì qù. 我们不会去。

3 You will not be going. Nǐ bù huì qù de. 你不会去的。

4 You will not be going. Nǐ bù huì qù de. 你不会去的。

5 He will not be going. Tā bù huì qù de. 他不会去的。

6 She will not be going. Tā bù huì qù de. 她不会去的。

7 It will not be going. Tā bù huì qù. 它不会去。

8 Ridhaan will not be going. Ridhaan bù huì qù. Ridhaan 不会去。

9 They will not be going. Tāmen bù huì qù de. 他们不会去的。

10 Children will not be going. Háizimen bù huì qù. 孩子们不会去。

1 I will not be writing. Wǒ bù huì xiězuò. 我不会写作。

2 We will not be writing. Wǒmen bù huì xiězuò. 我们不会写作。

3 You will not be writing. Nǐ bù huì xiězuò. 你不会写作。

4 You will not be writing. Nǐ bù huì xiězuò. 你不会写作。

5 He will not be writing. Tā bù huì xiězuò. 他不会写作。

6 She will not be writing. Tā bù huì xiězuò. 她不会写作。

7 It will not be writing. Tā bù huì xiě. 它不会写。

8 Ridhaan will not be writing. Ridhaan bù huì xiězuò. Ridhaan 不会写作。

9 They will not be writing. Tāmen bù huì xiězuò. 他们不会写作。

10 Children will not be writing. Háizi bù huì xiě. 孩子不会写。

1 I will not have gone. Wǒ bù huì zǒule. 我不会走了。

2 We will not have gone. Wǒmen bù huì zǒule. 我们不会走了。

3 You will not have gone. Nǐ bù huì zǒule. 你不会走了。

4 You will not have gone. Nǐ bù huì zǒule. 你不会走了。

5 He will not have gone. Tā bù huì zǒule. 他不会走了。

6 She will not have gone. Tā bù huì zǒule. 她不会走了。

7 It will not have gone. Tā bù huì xiāoshī. 它不会消失。

8 Ridhaan will not have gone. Ridhaan bù huì líkāi. Ridhaan不会离开。

9 They will not have gone. Tāmen bù huì zǒule. 他们不会走了。

10 Children will not have gone. Háizimen bù huì zǒule. 孩子们不会走了。

1 I will not have written. Wǒ bù huì xiě de. 我不会写的。

2 We will not have written. Wǒmen bù huì xiě. 我们不会写。

3 You will not have written. Nǐ bù huì xiě de. 你不会写的。

4 You will not have written. Nǐ bù huì xiě de. 你不会写的。

5 He will not have written. Tā bù huì xiě de. 他不会写的。

6 She will not have written. Tā bù huì xiě de. 她不会写的。

7 It will not have written. Tā bù huì xiě. 它不会写。

8 Ridhaan will not have written. Ridhaan bù huì xiě de. Ridhaan 不会写的。

9 They will not have written. Tāmen bù huì xiě. 他们不会写。

10 Children will not have written. Háizi bù huì xiě. 孩子不会写。

1 I can not go. Wǒ bùnéng qù. 我不能去。

2 We can not go. Wǒmen bùnéng qù. 我们不能去。

3 You can not go. Nǐ bùnéng qù. 你不能去。

4 You can not go. Nǐ bùnéng qù. 你不能去。

5 He can not go. Tā bùnéng qù. 他不能去。

6 She can not go. Tā bùnéng qù. 她不能去。

7 It can not go. Tā bùnéng qù. 它不能去。

8 Ridhaan can not go. Ridhaan bùnéng qù. Ridhaan不能去。

9 They can not go. Tāmen bùnéng qù. 他们不能去。

10 Children can not go. Háizi bùnéng qù. 孩子不能去。

1 I can not write. Wǒ bùnéng xiě. 我不能写。

2 We can not write. Wǒmen bùnéng xiě. 我们不能写。

3 You can not write. Nǐ bùnéng xiě. 你不能写。

4 You can not write. Nǐ bùnéng xiě. 你不能写。

5 He can not write. Tā bùnéng xiě. 他不能写。

6 She can not write. Tā bù huì xiě. 她不会写。

7 It can not write. Tā bùnéng xiě. 它不能写。

8 Ridhaan can not write. Ridhaan bùnéng xiě. Ridhaan 不能写。

9 They can not write. Tāmen bùnéng xiě. 他们不能写。

10 Children can not write. Háizi bù huì xiě. 孩子不会写。

1 I could not go. Wǒ bùnéng qù. 我不能去。

2 We could not go. Wǒmen bùnéng qù. 我们不能去。

3 You could not go. Nǐ bùnéng qù. 你不能去。

4 You could not go. Nǐ bùnéng qù. 你不能去。

5 He could not go. Tā bùnéng qù. 他不能去。

6 She could not go. Tā bùnéng qù. 她不能去。

7 It could not go. Tā bùnéng qù. 它不能去。

8 Ridhaan could not go. Ridhaan bùnéng qù. Ridhaan不能去。

9 They could not go. Tāmen bùnéng qù. 他们不能去。

10 Children could not go. Háizimen bùnéng qù. 孩子们不能去。

1 I could not write. Wǒ xiě bù chū. 我写不出。

2 We could not write. Wǒmen bùnéng xiě. 我们不能写。

3 You could not write. Nǐ bùnéng xiě. 你不能写。

4 You could not write. Nǐ bùnéng xiě. 你不能写。

5 He could not write. Tā bùnéng xiě. 他不能写。

6 She could not write. Tā bù huì xiě. 她不会写。

7 It could not write. Tā xiě bù chūlái. 它写不出来。

8 Ridhaan could not write. Ridhaan bùnéng xiě. Ridhaan 不能写。

9 They could not write. Tāmen bùnéng xiě. 他们不能写。

10 Children could not write. Háizimen bù huì xiě. 孩子们不会写。

1 Do I go?. Wǒ qù ma?. 我去吗？。

2 Do we go?. Wǒmen qù ma?. 我们去吗？。

3 Do you go?. Nǐ yǒu qù?. 你有去？。

4 Do you go?. Nǐ yǒu qù?. 你有去？。

5 Does he go?. Tā qù ma?. 他去吗？。

6 Does she go?. Tā qù ma?. 她去吗？。

7 Does it go?. Qùle ma?. 去了吗？。

8 Does Ridhaan go?. Ridhaan qù ma? Ridhaan去吗？

9 Do they go?. Tāmen qù ma?. 他们去吗？。

10 Do children go?. Háizi qù ma? 孩子去吗？

1 Do I write?. Wǒ xiě ma?. 我写吗？。

2 Do we write?. Wǒmen xiě?. 我们写？。

3 Do you write?. Nǐ xiě ma?. 你写吗？。

4 Do you write?. Nǐ xiě ma?. 你写吗？。

5 Does he write?. Tā huì xiě ma?. 他会写吗？。

6 Does she write?. Tā huì xiě ma?. 她会写吗？。

7 Does it write?. Huì xiě ma?. 会写吗？。

8 Does Ridhaan write?. Ridhaan huì xiě ma? Ridhaan 会写吗？

9 Do they write?. Tāmen xiě ma?. 他们写吗？。

10 Do children write?. Háizi huì xiě ma? 孩子会写吗？

1 AM I going?. Wǒ qù ma?. 我去吗？。

2 Are we going?. Wǒmen qù ma?. 我们去吗？。

3 Are you going?. Nǐ yào qù ma?. 你要去吗？。

4 Are you going?. Nǐ yào qù ma?. 你要去吗？。
5 Is he going?. Tā yào qù ma?. 他要去吗？。
6 Is she going?. Tā yào qù ma?. 她要去吗？。
7 Is it going?. Qùle ma.. 去了吗。。
8 Is Ridhaan going?. Ridhaan yào qù ma? Ridhaan要去吗？
9 Are they going?. Tāmen yào qù ma?. 他们要去吗？。
10 Are children going?. Háizimen qù ma? 孩子们去吗？
1 AM I writing?. Wǒ zài xiě ma?. 我在写吗？。
2 Are we writing?. Wǒmen zài xiězuò ma?. 我们在写作吗？。
3 Are you writing?. Nǐ zài xiě ma?. 你在写吗？。
4 Are you writing?. Nǐ zài xiě ma?. 你在写吗？。
5 Is he writing?. Tā zài xiě ma?. 他在写吗？。
6 Is she writing?. Tā zài xiě ma?. 她在写吗？。
7 Is it writing?. Shì xiě ma.. 是写吗。。
8 Is Ridhaan writing?. Ridhaan zài xiě ma? Ridhaan 在写吗？
9 Are they writing?. Tāmen zài xiě ma?. 他们在写吗？。
10 Are children writing?. Háizi zài xiě ma? 孩子在写吗？
1 Have I gone?. Wǒ qùle ma?. 我去了吗？。
2 Have we gone?. Wǒmen zǒule ma?. 我们走了吗？。
3 Have you gone?. Nǐ qùle ma?. 你去了吗？。
4 Have you gone?. Nǐ qùle ma?. 你去了吗？。
5 Has he gone?. Tā zǒule ma?. 他走了吗？。
6 Has she gone?. Tā zǒule ma?. 她走了吗？。
7 Has it gone?. Guòqùle ma.. 过去了吗。。
8 Has Ridhaan gone?. Ridhaan zǒule ma? Ridhaan走了吗？
9 Have they gone?. Tāmen zǒule ma?. 他们走了吗？。
10 Have children gone?. Háizimen zǒule ma? 孩子们走了吗？
1 Have I written?. Wǒ xiěle ma?. 我写了吗？。
2 Have we written?. Wǒmen xiěle ma? 我们写了吗？
3 Have you written?. Xiěle ma.. 写了吗。。
4 Have you written?. Xiěle ma.. 写了吗。。
5 Has he written?. Tā xiěle ma?. 他写了吗？。
6 Has she written?. Tā xiěle ma? 她写了吗？
7 Has it written?. Xiěle ma.. 写了吗。。

8 Has Ridhaan written?. Ridhaan xiěle ma? Ridhaan 写了吗？

9 Have they written?. Tāmen xiěle ma? 他们写了吗？

10 Have children written?. Yǒu háizi xiě ma? 有孩子写吗？

1 Did I go?. Wǒ qùle ma?. 我去了吗？。

2 Did we go?. Wǒmen qùle ma?. 我们去了吗？。

3 Did you go?. Nǐ qùle ma?. 你去了吗？。

4 Did you go?. Nǐ qùle ma?. 你去了吗？。

5 Did he go?. Tā qùle ma?. 他去了吗？。

6 Did she go?. Tā qùle ma?. 她去了吗？。

7 Did it go?. Qùle ma.. 去了吗。。

8 Did Ridhaan go?. Ridhaan qùle ma? Ridhaan去了吗？

9 Did they go?. Tāmen qùle ma? 他们去了吗？

10 Did children go?. Háizi qùle ma? 孩子去了吗？

1 Did I write?. Wǒ xiěle ma?. 我写了吗？。

2 Did we write?. Wǒmen xiěle ma? 我们写了吗？

3 Did you write?. Nǐ xiěle ma?. 你写了吗？。

4 Did you write?. Nǐ xiěle ma?. 你写了吗？。

5 Did he write?. Tā xiěle ma?. 他写了吗？。

6 Did she write?. Tā xiě de?. 她写的？。

7 Did it write?. Xiěle ma.. 写了吗。。

8 Did Ridhaan write?. Ridhaan xiě de ma? Ridhaan 写的吗？

9 Did they write?. Tāmen xiěle ma?. 他们写了吗？。

10 Did children write?. Háizimen xiěle ma? 孩子们写了吗？

1 Was I going?. Wǒ qù ma?. 我去吗？。

2 Were we going?. Wǒmen qù ma?. 我们去吗？。

3 Were you going?. Nǐ qùle ma?. 你去了吗？。

4 Were you going?. Nǐ qùle ma?. 你去了吗？。

5 Was he going?. Tā yào qù ma? 他要去吗？

6 was she going?. Tā yào qù ma? 她要去吗？

7 Was it going?. Qùle ma? 去了吗？

8 Was Ridhaan going?. Ridhaan qùle ma? Ridhaan去了吗？

9 Were they going?. Tāmen yào qù ma? 他们要去吗？

10 were children going?. Háizimen qù ma? 孩子们去吗？

1 Was I writing?. Wǒ zài xiě ma?. 我在写吗？。

2 Were we writing?. Wǒmen zài xiězuò ma? 我们在写作吗？

3 Were you writing?. Nǐ zài xiě ma?. 你在写吗？。

4 Were you writing?. Nǐ zài xiě ma?. 你在写吗？。

5 Was he writing?. Tā zài xiě ma? 他在写吗？

6 Was she writing?. Tā zài xiě ma? 她在写吗？

7 Was it writing?. Shì xiě de ma?. 是写的吗？。

8 Was Ridhaan writing?. Ridhaan zài xiě ma? Ridhaan 在写吗？

9 Were they writing?. Tāmen zài xiě ma? 他们在写吗？

10 Were children writing?. Háizimen zài xiě ma? 孩子们在写吗？

1 Will I go?. Wǒ huì qù ma?. 我会去吗？。

2 Will we go?. Wǒmen huì qù ma?. 我们会去吗？。

3 Will you go?. Nǐ huì qù ma?. 你会去吗？。

4 Will you go?. Nǐ huì qù ma?. 你会去吗？。

5 Will he go?. Tā huì qù ma?. 他会去吗？。

6 Will she go?. Tā huì qù ma?. 她会去吗？。

7 Will it go?. Huì qù ma?. 会去吗？。

8 Will Ridhaan go?. Ridhaan huì qù ma? Ridhaan会去吗？

9 Will they go?. Tāmen huì qù ma?. 他们会去吗？。

10 Will children go?. Háizi huì qù ma? 孩子会去吗？

1 Will I write?. Wǒ huì xiě ma?. 我会写吗？。

2 Will we write?. Wǒmen huì xiě ma?. 我们会写吗？。

3 Will you write?. Nǐ huì xiě ma?. 你会写吗？。

4 Will you write?. Nǐ huì xiě ma?. 你会写吗？。

5 Will he write?. Tā huì xiě ma?. 他会写吗？。

6 Will she write?. Tā huì xiě ma? 她会写吗？

7 Will it write?. Huì xiě ma.. 会写吗。。

8 Will Ridhaan write?. Ridhaan huì xiě ma? Ridhaan 会写吗？

9 Will they write?. Tāmen huì xiě ma? 他们会写吗？

10 Will children write?. Háizi huì xiě ma? 孩子会写吗？

1 Will I be going?. Wǒ huì qù ma?. 我会去吗？。

2 Will we be going?. Wǒmen huì qù ma?. 我们会去吗？。

3 Will you be going?. Nǐ huì qù ma?. 你会去吗？。

4 Will you be going?. Nǐ huì qù ma?. 你会去吗？。

5 Will he be going?. Tā huì qù ma?. 他会去吗？。

6 Will she be going?. Tā huì qù ma?. 她会去吗？。

7 Will it be going?. Huì qù ma.. 会去吗。。

8 Will Ridhaan be going?. Ridhaan huì qù ma? Ridhaan会去吗？

9 Will they be going?. Tāmen huì qù ma?. 他们会去吗？。

10 Will children be going?. Háizi huì qù ma? 孩子会去吗？

1 Will I be writing?. Wǒ huì xiě ma?. 我会写吗？。

2 Will we be writing?. Wǒmen huì xiězuò ma? 我们会写作吗？

3 Will you be writing?. Nǐ huì xiě ma?. 你会写吗？。

4 Will you be writing?. Nǐ huì xiě ma?. 你会写吗？。

5 Will he be writing?. Tā huì xiězuò ma? 他会写作吗？

6 Will she be writing?. Tā huì xiězuò ma? 她会写作吗？

7 Will it be writing?. Huì bù huì xiě?. 会不会写？。

8 Will Ridhaan be writing?. Ridhaan huì xiězuò ma? Ridhaan 会写作吗？

9 Will they be writing?. Tāmen huì xiězuò ma? 他们会写作吗？

10 Will children be writing?. Háizi huì xiě ma? 孩子会写吗？

1 Will I have gone?. Wǒ huì qù ma?. 我会去吗？。

2 Will we have gone?. Wǒmen huì zǒule ma?. 我们会走了吗？。

3 Will you have gone?. Nǐ huì qù ma?. 你会去吗？。

4 Will you have gone?. Nǐ huì qù ma?. 你会去吗？。

5 Will he have gone?. Tā huì zǒule ma?. 他会走了吗？。

6 Will she have gone?. Tā huì zǒule ma?. 她会走了吗？。

7 Will it have gone?. Huì guòqù ma?. 会过去吗？。

8 Will Ridhaan have gone?. Ridhaan huì líkāi ma? Ridhaan会离开吗？

9 Will they have gone?. Tāmen huì zǒule ma?. 他们会走了吗？。

10 Will children have gone?. Háizi huì bù huì zǒule? 孩子会不会走了？

1 Will I have written?. Wǒ huì xiě ma?. 我会写吗？。

2 Will we have written?. Wǒmen huì xiě ma? 我们会写吗？

3 Will you have written?. Nǐ huì xiě ma?. 你会写吗？。

4 Will you have written?. Nǐ huì xiě ma?. 你会写吗？。

5 Will he have written?. Tā huì xiě ma? 他会写吗？

6 Will she have written?. Tā huì xiě ma? 她会写吗？

7 Will it have written?. Huì xiě ma?. 会写吗？。

8 Will Ridhaan have written?. Ridhaan huì xiě ma? Ridhaan 会写吗？

9 Will they have written?. Tāmen huì xiě ma? 他们会写吗？

10 Will children have written?. Háizi huì bù huì xiě? 孩子会不会写？
1 Can I go?. Wǒ kěyǐ qù ma?. 我可以去吗？。
2 Can we go?. Wǒmen kěyǐ qù ma?. 我们可以去吗？。
3 Can you go?. Nǐ kěyǐ qù ma?. 你可以去吗？。
4 Can you go?. Nǐ kěyǐ qù ma?. 你可以去吗？。
5 Can he go?. Tā néng qù ma?. 他能去吗？。
6 Can she go?. Tā kěyǐ qù ma?. 她可以去吗？。
7 Can it go?. Kěyǐ qù ma?. 可以去吗？。
8 Can Ridhaan go?. Ridhaan kěyǐ qù ma? Ridhaan可以去吗？
9 Can they go?. Tāmen kěyǐ qù ma? 他们可以去吗？
10 Can children go?. Hái zǐ kěyǐ qù ma? 孩子可以去吗？
1 Can I write?. Kěyǐ xiě ma.. 可以写吗。。
2 Can we write?. Wǒmen kěyǐ xiě ma?. 我们可以写吗？。
3 Can you write?. Nǐ néng xiě ma?. 你能写吗？。
4 Can you write?. Nǐ néng xiě ma?. 你能写吗？。
5 Can he write?. Tā huì xiě ma?. 他会写吗？。
6 Can she write?. Tā huì xiě ma?. 她会写吗？。
7 Can it write?. Néng xiě ma.. 能写吗。。
8 Can Ridhaan write?. Ridhaan huì xiě ma? Ridhaan 会写吗？
9 Can they write?. Tāmen huì xiě ma?. 他们会写吗？。
10 Can children write?. Háizi huì xiě ma? 孩子会写吗？
1 Could I go?. Wǒ kěyǐ qù ma?. 我可以去吗？。
2 Could we go?. Wǒmen kěyǐ qù ma? 我们可以去吗？
3 Could you go?. Nǐ néng qù ma?. 你能去吗？。
4 Could you go?. Nǐ néng qù ma?. 你能去吗？。
5 Could he go?. Tā néng qù ma?. 他能去吗？。
6 Could she go?. Tā néng qù ma? 她能去吗？
7 Could it go?. Kěyǐ qù ma?. 可以去吗？。
8 Could Ridhaan go?. Ridhaan kěyǐ qù ma? Ridhaan可以去吗？
9 Could they go?. Tāmen kěyǐ qù ma? 他们可以去吗？
10 Could children go?. Hái zǐ kěyǐ qù ma? 孩子可以去吗？
1 Could I write?. Wǒ kěyǐ xiě ma?. 我可以写吗？。
2 Could we write?. Wǒmen kěyǐ xiě ma? 我们可以写吗？
3 Could you write?. Néng xiě ma.. 能写吗。。

4 Could you write?. Néng xiě ma.. 能写吗。。
5 Could he write?. Tā huì xiě ma?. 他会写吗？。
6 Could she write?. Tā huì xiě ma? 她会写吗？
7 Could it write?. Néng xiě ma.. 能写吗。。
8 Could Ridhaan write?. Ridhaan huì xiě ma? Ridhaan 会写吗？
9 Could they write?. Tāmen néng xiě ma? 他们能写吗？
10 Could children write?. Háizi huì xiě ma? 孩子会写吗？
1 Do I not go?. Wǒ bù qù ma?. 我不去吗？。
2 Do we not go?. Wǒmen bù qù ma?. 我们不去吗？。
3 Do you not go?. Nǐ bù qù ma?. 你不去吗？。
4 Do you not go?. Nǐ bù qù ma?. 你不去吗？。
5 Does he not go?. Tā bù qù ma?. 他不去吗？。
6 Does she not go?. Tā bù qù ma? 她不去吗？
7 Does it not go?. Bù qù ma?. 不去吗？。
8 Does Ridhaan not go?. Ridhaan bù qù ma? Ridhaan 不去吗？
9 Do they not go?. Tāmen bù qù ma? 他们不去吗？
10 Do children not go?. Háizi bù qù ma? 孩子不去吗？
1 Do I not write?. Wǒ bù xiě?. 我不写？。
2 Do we not write?. Wǒmen bù xiě ma? 我们不写吗？
3 Do you not write?. Nǐ bù xiě ma?. 你不写吗？。
4 Do you not write?. Nǐ bù xiě ma?. 你不写吗？。
5 Does he not write?. Tā bù xiě ma?. 他不写吗？。
6 Does she not write?. Tā bù xiě ma? 她不写吗？
7 Does it not write?. Bù xiě ma?. 不写吗？。
8 Does Ridhaan not write?. Ridhaan bù xiě ma? Ridhaan 不写吗？
9 Do they not write?. Tāmen bù xiě ma? 他们不写吗？
10 Do children not write?. Háizi bù xiě ma? 孩子不写吗？
1 AM I not going?. Wǒ bù qù ma?. 我不去吗？。
2 Are we not going?. Wǒmen bù qù ma?. 我们不去吗？。
3 Are you not going?. Nǐ bù qù ma?. 你不去吗？。
4 Are you not going?. Nǐ bù qù ma?. 你不去吗？。
5 Is he not going?. Tā bù qù ma?. 他不去吗？。
6 Is she not going?. Tā bù qù ma?. 她不去吗？。
7 Is it not going?. Bù qù ma?. 不去吗？。

8 Is Ridhaan not going?. Ridhaan bù qù ma? Ridhaan 不去吗？

9 Are they not going?. Tāmen bù qù ma?. 他们不去吗？。

10 Are children not going?. Háizi bù qù ma? 孩子不去吗？

1 AM I not writing?. Wǒ bùshì zài xiě ma?. 我不是在写吗？。

2 Are we not writing?. Wǒmen bùshì zài xiě ma? 我们不是在写吗？

3 Are you not writing?. Nǐ bù xiě?. 你不写？。

4 Are you not writing?. Nǐ bù xiě?. 你不写？。

5 Is he not writing?. Tā bùshì zài xiě ma? 他不是在写吗？

6 Is she not writing?. Tā bùshì zài xiě ma? 她不是在写吗？

7 Is it not writing?. Bùshì zài xiě ma?. 不是在写吗？。

8 Is Ridhaan not writing?. Ridhaan bù xiě ma? Ridhaan 不写吗？

9 Are they not writing?. Tāmen bù xiě ma? 他们不写吗？

10 Are children not writing?. Háizi bù xiězì? 孩子不写字？

1 Have I not gone?. Wǒ méiyǒu qù ma?. 我没有去吗？。

2 Have we not gone?. Wǒmen bùshì zǒule ma?. 我们不是走了吗？。

3 Have you not gone?. Nǐ méiyǒu qù ma?. 你没有去吗？。

4 Have you not gone?. Nǐ méiyǒu qù ma?. 你没有去吗？。

5 Has he not gone?. Tā bùshì zǒule ma?. 他不是走了吗？。

6 Has she not gone?. Tā bùshì zǒule ma?. 她不是走了吗？。

7 Has it not gone?. Shì bùshì méiliǎo?. 是不是没了？。

8 Has Ridhaan not gone?. Ridhaan méiyǒu zǒu ma? Ridhaan没有走吗？

9 Have they not gone?. Tāmen méiyǒu zǒu ma?. 他们没有走吗？。

10 Have children not gone?. Hái zǐ huán méi zǒu? 孩子还没走？

1 Have I not written?. Wǒ méiyǒu xiě ma?. 我没有写吗？。

2 Have we not written?. Wǒmen méiyǒu xiě ma? 我们没有写吗？

3 Have you not written?. Méi xiě ma.. 没写吗。。

4 Have you not written?. Méi xiě ma.. 没写吗。。

5 Has he not written?. Tā méiyǒu xiě ma? 他没有写吗？

6 Has she not written?. Tā méiyǒu xiě ma? 她没有写吗？

7 Has it not written?. Méi xiě ma.. 没写吗。。

8 Has Ridhaan not written?. Ridhaan méiyǒu xiě ma? Ridhaan 没有写吗？

9 Have they not written?. Tāmen méiyǒu xiě ma? 他们没有写吗？

10 Have children not written?. Yǒu háizi méi xiě ma? 有孩子没写吗？

1 Did I not go?. Wǒ méi qù ma?. 我没去吗？。

2 Did we not go?. Wǒmen méiyǒu qù ma?. 我们没有去吗？。

3 Did you not go?. Nǐ méi qù ma?. 你没去吗？。

4 Did you not go?. Nǐ méi qù ma?. 你没去吗？。

5 Did he not go?. Tā méi qù ma?. 他没去吗？。

6 Did she not go?. Tā méi qù ma? 她没去吗？

7 Did it not go?. Méi qù ma?. 没去吗？。

8 Did Ridhaan not go?. Ridhaan méiyǒu qù ma? Ridhaan没有去吗？

9 Did they not go?. Tāmen méiyǒu qù ma?. 他们没有去吗？。

10 Did children not go?. Háizi méi qù ma? 孩子没去吗？

1 Did I not write?. Wǒ méi xiě?. 我没写？。

2 Did we not write?. Wǒmen méiyǒu xiě ma? 我们没有写吗？

3 Did you not write?. Nǐ méi xiě?. 你没写？。

4 Did you not write?. Nǐ méi xiě?. 你没写？。

5 Did he not write?. Tā méiyǒu xiě ma?. 他没有写吗？。

6 Did she not write?. Tā méi xiě ma? 她没写吗？

7 Did it not write?. Méi xiě ma.. 没写吗。。

8 Did Ridhaan not write?. Ridhaan méiyǒu xiě ma? Ridhaan没有写吗？

9 Did they not write?. Tāmen méiyǒu xiě ma? 他们没有写吗？

10 Did children not write?. Háizi méi xiě? 孩子没写？

1 Was I not going?. Wǒ bù qù ma?. 我不去吗？。

2 Were we not going?. Wǒmen bù qù ma?. 我们不去吗？。

3 Were you not going?. Nǐ bù qù ma?. 你不去吗？。

4 Were you not going?. Nǐ bù qù ma?. 你不去吗？。

5 Was he not going?. Tā bù qù ma?. 他不去吗？。

6 was she not going?. Tā bù qù ma? 她不去吗？

7 Was it not going?. Bù qù ma?. 不去吗？。

8 Was Ridhaan not going?. Ridhaan bù qù ma? Ridhaan 不去吗？

9 Were they not going?. Tāmen bù qù ma? 他们不去吗？

10 were children not going?. Háizi men bù qù ma? 孩子们不去吗？

1 Was I not writing?. Wǒ bùshì zài xiě ma?. 我不是在写吗？。

2 Were we not writing?. Wǒmen bùshì zài xiě ma? 我们不是在写吗？

3 Were you not writing?. Nǐ bùshì zài xiě ma?. 你不是在写吗？。

4 Were you not writing?. Nǐ bùshì zài xiě ma?. 你不是在写吗？。

5 Was he not writing?. Tā bùshì zài xiě ma? 他不是在写吗？

6 Was she not writing?. Tā bùshì zài xiě ma? 她不是在写吗？

7 Was it not writing?. Bùshì zài xiě ma? 不是在写吗？

8 Was Ridhaan not writing?. Ridhaan bùshì zài xiězuò ma? Ridhaan 不是在写作吗？

9 Were they not writing?. Tāmen bùshì zài xiě ma? 他们不是在写吗？

10 Were children not writing?. Háizi bù huì xiězì ma? 孩子不会写字吗？

1 Will I not go?. Wǒ bù qù ma?. 我不去吗？。

2 Will we not go?. Wǒmen bù qù ma?. 我们不去吗？。

3 Will you not go?. Nǐ bù qù ma?. 你不去吗？。

4 Will you not go?. Nǐ bù qù ma?. 你不去吗？。

5 Will he not go?. Tā bù huì qù ma?. 他不会去吗？。

6 Will she not go?. Tā bù huì qù ma? 她不会去吗？

7 Will it not go?. Bù huì qù ma?. 不会去吗？。

8 Will Ridhaan not go?. Ridhaan bù huì qù ma? Ridhaan 不会去吗？

9 Will they not go?. Tāmen bù huì qù ma?. 他们不会去吗？。

10 Will children not go?. Háizi bù huì qù ma? 孩子不会去吗？

1 Will I not write?. Wǒ bù huì xiě ma?. 我不会写吗？。

2 Will we not write?. Wǒmen bù huì xiě ma? 我们不会写吗？

3 Will you not write?. Nǐ bù huì xiě ma?. 你不会写吗？。

4 Will you not write?. Nǐ bù huì xiě ma?. 你不会写吗？。

5 Will he not write?. Tā bù huì xiě ma? 他不会写吗？

6 Will she not write?. Tā bù huì xiě ma? 她不会写吗？

7 Will it not write?. Huì bù huì xiě?. 会不会写？。

8 Will Ridhaan not write?. Ridhaan bù huì xiě ma? Ridhaan 不会写吗？

9 Will they not write?. Tāmen bù huì xiě ma? 他们不会写吗？

10 Will children not write?. Háizi bù huì xiě ma? 孩子不会写吗？

1 Will I not be going?. Wǒ bù huì qù ma?. 我不会去吗？。

2 Will we not be going?. Wǒmen bù huì qù ma?. 我们不会去吗？。

3 Will you not be going?. Nǐ bù qù ma?. 你不去吗？。

4 Will you not be going?. Nǐ bù qù ma?. 你不去吗？。

5 Will he not be going?. Tā bù huì qù ma?. 他不会去吗？。

6 Will she not be going?. Tā bù huì qù ma?. 她不会去吗？。

7 Will it not be going?. Bù huì qù ba?. 不会去吧？。

8 Will Ridhaan not be going?. Ridhaan bù huì qù ma? Ridhaan 不会去吗？

9 Will they not be going?. Tāmen bù huì qù ma? 他们不会去吗？

10 Will children not be going?. Háizi bù huì qù ma? 孩子不会去吗？

1 Will I not be writing?. Wǒ bù huì xiě ma?. 我不会写吗？。

2 Will we not be writing?. Wǒmen bù huì xiězuò ma? 我们不会写作吗？

3 Will you not be writing?. Nǐ bù huì xiě ma? 你不会写吗？

4 Will you not be writing?. Nǐ bù huì xiě ma? 你不会写吗？

5 Will he not be writing?. Tā bù huì xiězuò ma? 他不会写作吗？

6 Will she not be writing?. Tā bù huì xiězuò ma? 她不会写作吗？

7 Will it not be writing?. Bù huì xiě ba? 不会写吧？

8 Will Ridhaan not be writing?. Ridhaan bù huì xiězuò ma? Ridhaan 不会写作吗？

9 Will they not be writing?. Tāmen bù huì xiězuò ma? 他们不会写作吗？

10 Will children not be writing?. Háizi huì bù huì xiězì? 孩子会不会写字？

1 Will I not have gone?. Wǒ bù huì zǒule ma?. 我不会走了吗？。

2 Will we not have gone?. Wǒmen bù huì yǐjīng zǒule?. 我们不会已经走了？。

3 Will you not have gone?. Nǐ bù huì qù ma?. 你不会去吗？。

4 Will you not have gone?. Nǐ bù huì qù ma?. 你不会去吗？。

5 Will he not have gone?. Tā bù huì zǒule ma?. 他不会走了吗？。

6 Will she not have gone?. Tā bù huì zǒu ba? 她不会走吧？

7 Will it not have gone?. Tā bù huì xiāoshī ma?. 它不会消失吗？。

8 Will Ridhaan not have gone?. Ridhaan bù huì zǒule ma? Ridhaan 不会走了吗？

9 Will they not have gone?. Tāmen bù huì zǒule ma?. 他们不会走了吗？。

10 Will children not have gone?. Huì bù huì háizi dōu zǒule? 会不会孩子都走了？

1 Will I not have written?. Wǒ bù huì xiě ma?. 我不会写吗？。

2 Will we not have written?. Wǒmen bù huì xiě ma? 我们不会写吗？

3 Will you not have written?. Nǐ bù huì xiě ma?. 你不会写吗？。

4 Will you not have written?. Nǐ bù huì xiě ma?. 你不会写吗？。

5 Will he not have written?. Tā huì bù huì méiyǒu xiě? 他会不会没有写？

6 Will she not have written?. Tā bù huì xiě ba? 她不会写吧？

7 Will it not have written?. Huì bù huì méiyǒu xiě? 会不会没有写？

8 Will Ridhaan not have written?. Ridhaan bù huì xiě ma? Ridhaan 不会写吗？

9 Will they not have written?. Tāmen bù huì xiě ma? 他们不会写吗？

10 Will children not have written?. Huì bù huì háizi bù huì xiě? 会不会孩子不会写？

1 Can I not go?. Wǒ kěyǐ bù qù ma?. 我可以不去吗？。

2 Can we not go?. Wǒmen kěyǐ bù qù ma?. 我们可以不去吗？。

3 Can you not go?. Kěyǐ bù qù ma?. 可以不去吗？。

4 Can you not go?. Kěyǐ bù qù ma?. 可以不去吗？。

5 Can he not go?. Tā kěyǐ bù qù ma?. 他可以不去吗？。

6 Can she not go?. Tā kěyǐ bù qù ma? 她可以不去吗？

7 Can it not go?. Kěyǐ bù qù ma?. 可以不去吗？。

8 Can Ridhaan not go?. Ridhaan kěyǐ bù qù ma? Ridhaan可以不去吗？

9 Can they not go?. Tāmen bùnéng qù ma? 他们不能去吗？

10 Can children not go?. Hái zǐ kěyǐ bù qù ma? 孩子可以不去吗？

1 Can I not write?. Kěyǐ bù xiě ma?. 可以不写吗？。

2 Can we not write?. Kěyǐ bù xiě ma? 可以不写吗？

3 Can you not write?. Kěyǐ bù xiě ma?. 可以不写吗？。

4 Can you not write?. Kěyǐ bù xiě ma?. 可以不写吗？。

5 Can he not write?. Tā bùnéng xiě ma? 他不能写吗？

6 Can she not write?. Tā bùnéng xiě ma? 她不能写吗？

7 Can it not write?. Kěyǐ bù xiě ma?. 可以不写吗？。

8 Can Ridhaan not write?. Ridhaan kěyǐ bù xiě ma? Ridhaan 可以不写吗？

9 Can they not write?. Tāmen bùnéng xiě ma? 他们不能写吗？

10 Can children not write?. Háizi bù huì xiězì? 孩子不会写字？

1 Could I not go?. Wǒ kěyǐ bù qù ma?. 我可以不去吗？。

2 Could we not go?. Wǒmen kěyǐ bù qù ma?. 我们可以不去吗？。

3 Could you not go?. Nǐ kěyǐ bù qù ma?. 你可以不去吗？。

4 Could you not go?. Nǐ kěyǐ bù qù ma?. 你可以不去吗？。

5 Could he not go?. Tā néng bù qù ma?. 他能不去吗？。

6 Could she not go?. Tā bùnéng qù ma? 她不能去吗？

7 Could it not go?. Kěyǐ bù qù ma?. 可以不去吗？。

8 Could Ridhaan not go?. Ridhaan kěyǐ bù qù ma? Ridhaan 可以不去吗？

9 Could they not go?. Tāmen bùnéng qù ma? 他们不能去吗？

10 Could children not go?. Háizi bùnéng qù ma? 孩子不能去吗？

1 Could I not write?. Wǒ kěyǐ bù xiě ma?. 我可以不写吗？。

2 Could we not write?. Kěyǐ bù xiě ma? 可以不写吗？

3 Could you not write?. Kěyǐ bù xiě ma?. 可以不写吗？。

4 Could you not write?. Kěyǐ bù xiě ma?. 可以不写吗？。

5 Could he not write?. Tā néng bù xiě ma? 他能不写吗？

6 Could she not write?. Tā néng bù xiě ma? 她能不写吗？

7 Could it not write?. Kěyǐ bù xiě ma?. 可以不写吗？。

8 Could Ridhaan not write?. Ridhaan kěyǐ bù xiě ma? Ridhaan 可以不写吗？

9 Could they not write?. Tāmen bùnéng xiě ma? 他们不能写吗？

10 Could children not write?. Háizi bù huì xiě ma? 孩子不会写吗？

Chapter 3

Type 1

1 I do. Wǒ zuò. 我做。

2 I don't do Wǒ bù zuò 我不做

3 Do I do? wǒ zuò ma? 我做吗？

4 Do I not do? Wǒ bù zuò ma? 我不做吗？

5 I do, don't I? Wǒ zuò, bùshì ma? 我做，不是吗？

6 I don't do, do I? Wǒ bù zuò, shì ma? 我不做，是吗？

7 What do I do? Wǒ gāi zěnme bàn? 我该怎么办？

8 What do I not do? Wǒ bù zuò shénme? 我不做什么？

9 Why do I do? Wǒ wèishéme yào zhèyàng zuò? 我为什么要这样做？

10 Why do I not do? Wèishéme wǒ bù zuò? 为什么我不做？

11 How do I do? Wǒ gāi zěnme bàn? 我该怎么办？

12 How do I not do? Wǒ bùxíng zěnme bàn? 我不行怎么办？

13 When do I do? Wǒ shénme shíhòu zuò? 我什么时候做？

14 When do I not do? Wǒ shénme shíhòu bù zuò? 我什么时候不做？

15 Where do I do? Wǒ zài nǎlǐ zuò? 我在哪里做？

16 Where do I not do? Wǒ nǎlǐ bù zuò? 我哪里不做？

17 What do I do for? Wǒ zuò shénme? 我做什么？

18 What do I not do for? Wǒ bù zuò shénme? 我不做什么？

19 Whom do I do for? Wǒ wèi shéi zuò? 我为谁做？

20 Whom do I not do for? Wǒ bù wéi shéi zuò? 我不为谁做？

21 Whom do I do with? Wǒ hé shéi yīqǐ zuò? 我和谁一起做？

22 Whom do I not do with? Wǒ bù hé shéi zuò? 我不和谁做？

23 Who does? Shéi zuò? 谁做？

24 Who doesn't do? Shéi bù zuò? 谁不做？

25 Who do? Shéi zuò? 谁做？

26 Who don't do? Shéi bù zuò? 谁不做？

Type 2

1 I am doing. Wǒ zài zuò. 我在做。

2 I am not doing. Wǒ bùshì zài zuò. 我不是在做。

3 AM I doing? Wǒ zài zuò shénme? 我在做什么？

4 AM I not doing? Wǒ bùshì zài zuò ma? 我不是在做吗？

5 I am doing, am I not? Wǒ zài zuò, bùshì ma? 我在做，不是吗？

6 I am not doing, am I? Wǒ bùshì zài zuò, shì ma? 我不是在做，是吗？

7 What am I doing? Wǒ zài zuò shénme? 我在做什么？

8 What am I not doing? Wǒ bù zuò shénme? 我不做什么？

9 Why am I doing? Wǒ wèishéme yào zhèyàng zuò? 我为什么要这样做？

10 Why am I not doing? Wèishéme wǒ bù zuò? 为什么我不做？

11 How am I doing? Wǒ hǎo ma? 我好吗？

12 How am I not doing? Wǒ zěnme bùxíng? 我怎么不行？

13 When am I doing? Wǒ shénme shíhòu gàn? 我什么时候干？

14 When am I not doing? Wǒ shénme shíhòu bù zuò? 我什么时候不做？

15 Where am I doing? Wǒ zài zuò shénme? 我在做什么？

16 Where am I not doing? Wǒ nǎlǐ bù gān? 我哪里不干？

17 What am I doing for? Wǒ shì wèile shénme? 我是为了什么？

18 What am I not doing for? Wǒ bùshì wèile shénme? 我不是为了什么？

19 Whom am I doing for? Wǒ zài wèi shéi zuòshì? 我在为谁做事？

20 Whom am I not doing for? Wǒ bùshì wèi shéi zuò de? 我不是为谁做的？

21 Whom am I doing with? Wǒ zài hé shéi yīqǐ zuò? 我在和谁一起做？

22 Whom am I not doing with? Wǒ bù hé shéi zài yīqǐ? 我不和谁在一起？

23 Who is doing? Shéi zài zuò shénme? 谁在做什么？

24 Who is not doing? Shéi bù gān? 谁不干？

25 Who are doing? Shéi zài zuò shénme? 谁在做什么？

26 Who are not doing? Shéi bù gān? 谁不干？

Type 3

1 I have done. Wǒ yǐjīng zuò hǎole. 我已经做好了。

2 I have not done. Wǒ méiyǒu zuòguò. 我没有做过。

3 Have I done? Wǒ zuò dàole ma? 我做到了**吗**？

4 Have I not done? Wǒ méiyǒu zuò ma? 我没有做**吗**？

5 I have done, haven't I? Wǒ yǐjīng wánchéngle, bùshì ma? 我已经完成了，不是**吗**？

6 I have not done, have I? Wǒ méiyǒu zuò, shì ma? 我没有做，是**吗**？

7 What have I done? Wǒ zuòle shénme? 我做了什么？

8 What have I not done? Wǒ hái méiyǒu zuò shénme? 我还没有做什么？

9 Why have I done? Wèishéme wǒ zuòle? **为**什么我做了？

10 Why have not done? Wèishéme méiyǒu zuò? **为**什么没有做？

11 How have I done? Wǒ zuò dé zěnme yàng? 我做得怎么样？

12 How have I not done? Wǒ zěnme méi zuò? 我怎么没做？

13 When have I done? Wǒ shénme shíhòu zuòguò? 我什么时候做过？

14 When have I not done? Wǒ shénme shíhòu méi zuòguò? 我什么时候没做过？

15 Where have I done? Wǒ zài nǎlǐ zuòguò? 我在哪里做过？

16 Where have I not done? Wǒ nǎlǐ méi zuò? 我哪里没做？

17 What have I done for? Wǒ zuòle shénme? 我做了什么？

18 What have I not done for? Wǒ méiyǒu zuò shénme? 我没有做什么？

19 Whom have I done for? Wǒ wèi shéi zuòguò? 我**为谁**做过？

20 Whom have I not done for? Wǒ méiyǒu wéi shéi zuòguò? 我没有**为谁**做过？

21 Whom have I done with? Wǒ hé shéi zuòguò? 我和**谁**做过？

22 Whom have I not done with? Wǒ hái méiyǒu duì shéi zuòguò? 我还没有对**谁**做过？

23 Who has done? Shéi zuòguò? **谁**做过？

24 Who has not done? Shéi méiyǒu zuòguò? **谁**没有做过？

25 Who have done? Shéi zuòguò? **谁**做过？

26 Who have not done? Shéi méiyǒu zuòguò? **谁**没有做过？

Type 4

1 I did. Wǒ zuò dàole. 我做到了。

2 I didn't do. Wǒ méiyǒu zuò. 我没有做。

3 Did I do? Wǒ zuòle ma? 我做了**吗**？

4 Did I not do? Wǒ méiyǒu zuò ma? 我没有做**吗**？

5 I did, didn't I? Wǒ zuò dàole, bùshì ma? 我做到了，不是**吗**？

6 I didn't do, did I? Wǒ méiyǒu zuò, shì ma? 我没有做，是吗？

7 What did I do? Wǒ zuòle shénme? 我做了什么？

8 What did I not do? Wǒ méiyǒu zuò shénme? 我没有做什么？

9 Why did I do? Wǒ wèishéme zhèyàng zuò? 我为什么这样做？

10 Why did I not do? Wèishéme wǒ méiyǒu zuò? 为什么我没有做？

11 How did I do? Wǒ shì zěnme zuò de? 我是怎么做的？

12 How did I not do? Wǒ zěnme méi zuò? 我怎么没做？

13 When did I do? Wǒ shénme shíhòu zuò de? 我什么时候做的？

14 When did I not do? Wǒ shénme shíhòu méiyǒu zuò? 我什么时候没有做？

15 Where did I do? Wǒ zài nǎlǐ zuò de? 我在哪里做的？

16 Where did I not do? Wǒ nǎlǐ méi zuò? 我哪里没做？

17 What did I do for? Wǒ zuòle shénme? 我做了什么？

18 What did I not do for? Wǒ méiyǒu zuò shénme? 我没有做什么？

19 Whom did I do for? Wǒ wèi shéi zuò de? 我为谁做的？

20 Whom did I not do for? Wǒ bùshì wèi shéi zuò de? 我不是为谁做的？

21 Whom did I do with? Wǒ hé shéi zuòle? 我和谁做了？

22 Whom did I not do with? Wǒ méi hé shéi zuò? 我没和谁做？

23 Who did? Shéi gàn de? 谁干的？

24 Who didn't do? Shéi méi zuòguò? 谁没做过？

25 Who did? Shéi gàn de? 谁干的？

26 Who didn't do? Shéi méi zuòguò? 谁没做过？

Type 5

1 I was doing. Wǒ zài zuò. 我在做。

2 I was not doing. Wǒ bùshì zài zuò. 我不是在做。

3 Was I doing? Wǒ zài zuò shénme? 我在做什么？

4 Was I not doing? Wǒ bùshì zài zuò ma? 我不是在做吗？

5 I was doing, wasn't I? Wǒ zài zuò, bùshì ma? 我在做，不是吗？

6 I was not doing, was I? Wǒ méiyǒu zuò, shì ma? 我没有做，是吗？

7 What was I doing? Wǒ zài zuò shénme? 我在做什么？

8 What was I not doing? Wǒ méiyǒu zuò shénme? 我没有做什么？

9 Why was I doing? Wǒ wèishéme yào zhèyàng zuò? 我为什么要这样做？

10 Why was I not doing? Wèishéme wǒ méiyǒu zuò? 为什么我没有做？

11 How was I doing? Wǒguò dé zěnme yàng? 我过得怎么样？

12 How was I not doing? Wǒ zěnme méi zuò? 我怎么没做？

13 When was I doing? Wǒ shénme shíhòu zuò de? 我什么时候做的？

14 When was I not doing? Wǒ shénme shíhòu bù zuò? 我什么时候不做？

15 Where was I doing? Wǒ zài zuò shénme? 我在做什么？

16 Where was I not doing? Wǒ nǎlǐ méi zuò? 我哪里没做？

17 What was I doing for? Wǒ shì wèile shénme? 我是**为**了什么？

18 What was I not doing for? Wǒ bùshì wèile shénme? 我不是**为**了什么？

19 Whom was I doing for? Wǒ wèi shéi zuò de? 我**为谁**做的？

20 Whom was I not doing for? Wǒ bùshì wèi shéi zuò de? 我不是**为谁**做的？

21 Whom was I doing with? Wǒ hé shéi yīqǐ zuò de? 我和**谁**一起做的？

22 Whom was I not doing with? Wǒ méiyǒu hé shéi yīqǐ zuò? 我没有和**谁**一起做？

23 Who was doing? Shì shéi gàn de? 是**谁**干的？

24 Who was not doing? Shéi méiyǒu zuò? **谁**没有做？

25 Who were doing? Shéi zài zuò shénme? **谁**在做什么？

26 Who were not doing? Shéi méiyǒu zuò? **谁**没有做？

Type 6

1 I will do. Wǒ huì zuò. 我会做。

2 I will not do. Wǒ bù huì. 我不会。

3 What will I do? Wǒ gāi zěnme bàn? 我**该**怎么办？

4 What will I not do? Wǒ bù huì zuò shénme? 我不会做什么？

5 I will do, will not I? Wǒ huì zuò de, bùshì ma? 我会做的，不是**吗**？

6 I will not do, will I? Wǒ bù huì zuò de, shì ma? 我不会做的，是**吗**？

7 What will I do? Wǒ gāi zěnme bàn? 我**该**怎么办？

8 What will I not do? Wǒ bù huì zuò shénme? 我不会做什么？

9 Why will I do? Wǒ wèishéme yào zhèyàng zuò? 我**为**什么要这样做？

10 Why will I not do? Wèishéme wǒ bù huì ne? **为**什么我不会呢？

11 How will I do? Wǒ huì zěnme zuò? 我会怎么做？

12 How will I not do? Wǒ bù huì zěnme bàn? 我不会怎么办？

13 When will I do? Wǒ shénme shíhòu zuò? 我什么时候做？

14 When will I not do? Wǒ shénme shíhòu bù zuò? 我什么时候不做？

15 Where will I do? Wǒ huì zài nǎlǐ zuò? 我会在哪里做？

16 Where will I not do? Wǒ nǎlǐ bù huì zuò? 我哪里不会做？

17 What will I do for? Wǒ yào zuò shénme? 我要做什么？

18 What will I not do for? Wǒ bù huì zuò shénme? 我不会做什么？

19 Whom will I do for? Wǒ huì wèi shéi zuò? 我会**为谁**做？

20 Whom will I not do for? Wǒ bù huì wèi shéi zuò? 我不会**为谁**做？

21 Whom will I do with? Wǒ huì hé shéi yīqǐ zuò? 我会和**谁**一起做？

22 Whom will I not do with? Wǒ bù huì hé shéi zuò? 我不会和**谁**做？

23 Who will do? Shéi lái zuò? **谁**来做？

24 Who will not do? Shéi bù huì ne? **谁**不会呢？

25 Who will do? Shéi lái zuò? **谁**来做？

26 Who will not do? Shéi bù huì ne? **谁**不会呢？

Type 7

1 I will be doing. Wǒ huì zuò de. 我会做的。

2 I will be not doing. Wǒ bù huì zuò de. 我不会做的。

3 Will I be doing? Wǒ huì zuò ma? 我会做**吗**？

4 Will I not be doing? Wǒ bù huì zuò ma? 我不会做**吗**？

5 I will be doing, wouldn't I? Wǒ huì zuò de, bùshì ma? 我会做的，不是**吗**？

6 I will not be doing, would I? Wǒ bù huì zuò de, shì ma? 我不会做的，是**吗**？

7 What will I be doing? Wǒ huì zuò shénme? 我会做什么？

8 What will I not be doing? Wǒ bù huì zuò shénme? 我不会做什么？

9 Why will I be doing? Wǒ wèishéme yào zuò? 我**为**什么要做？

10 Why will I not be doing? Wèishéme wǒ bù huì zuò? **为**什么我不会做？

11 How will I be doing? Wǒ huì zěnme yàng? 我会怎么样？

12 How will I not be doing? Wǒ zěnme huì bù huì ne? 我怎么会不会呢？

13 When will I be doing? Wǒ shénme shíhòu huì zuò? 我什么时候会做？

14 When will I not be doing? Wǒ shénme shíhòu bù zuò? 我什么时候不做？

15 Where will I be doing? Wǒ huì zài nǎlǐ zuò? 我会在哪里做？

16 Where will I not be doing? Wǒ bù huì qù nǎlǐ zuò? 我不会去哪里做？

17 What will I be doing for? Wǒ yào zuò shénme? 我要做什么？

18 What will I be not doing for? Wǒ bù zuò shénme? 我不做什么？

19 Whom will I be doing for? Wǒ huì wèi shéi zuòshì? 我会**为谁**做事？

20 Whom will I not be doing for? Wǒ bù huì wèi shéi zuòshì? 我不会**为谁**做事？

21 Whom will I be doing for?.Whom will I be doing with? Wǒ jiāng wèi shéi zuò?. Wǒ jiāng hé shéi yīqǐ zuò? 我将为谁做？。我将和谁一起做？

22 Whom will I not be doing with? Wǒ bù huì hé shéi yīqǐ zuò? 我不会和谁一起做？

23 Who will be doing? Shéi lái zuò? 谁来做？

24 Who will not be doing? Shéi bù huì zuò? 谁不会做？

25 Who will be doing? Shéi lái zuò? 谁来做？

26 Who will not be doing? Shéi bù huì zuò? 谁不会做？

Type 8

1 I will have done. Wǒ huì zuò dào de. 我会做到的。

2 I won't have done. Wǒ bù huì zuò de. 我不会做的。

3 Will I have done? Wǒ huì zuò ma? 我会做吗？

4 Have I won't done? Wǒ bù huì zuò ma? 我不会做吗？

5 I will have done, won't I? Wǒ huì zuò dào de, bùshì ma? 我会做到的，不是吗？

6 I won't have done, will I? Wǒ bù huì zuò de, shì ma? 我不会做的，是吗？

7 What will have I done? Wǒ huì zěnme zuò? 我会怎么做？

8 What will have I not done? Shénme shì wǒ méiyǒu zuò de? 什么是我没有做的？

9 Why will have I done? Wǒ wèishéme yào zhèyàng zuò? 我为什么要这样做？

10 Why will have I not done? Wèishéme wǒ méiyǒu zuò? 为什么我没有做？

11 How will have I done? Wǒ huì zěnme zuò? 我会怎么做？

12 How will have I not done? Wǒ zěnme huì méiyǒu zuò? 我怎么会没有做？

13 When will have I done? Wǒ shénme shíhòu wánchéng? 我什么时候完成？

14 When will have I not done? Wǒ shénme shíhòu méiyǒu wánchéng? 我什么时候没有完成？

15 Where will have I done? Wǒ huì zài nǎlǐ zuò? 我会在哪里做？

16 Where will have I not done? Wǒ nǎlǐ méiyǒu zuò? 我哪里没有做？

17 What will have I done for? Wǒ huì zuò shénme? 我会做什么？

18 What will have I not done for? Shénme shì wǒ méiyǒu zuò de? 什么是我没有做的？

19 Whom will have I done for? Wǒ huì wèi shéi zuò? 我会**为谁**做？

20 Whom will have I not done for? Wǒ méiyǒu wéi shéi zuòguò? 我没有**为谁**做过？

21 Whom will have I done with? Wǒ huì hé shéi zuò? 我会和**谁**做？

22 Whom will have I done? Wǒ huì zuò shéi? 我会做**谁**？

23 Who will have done? Shéi huì zuòguò? **谁**会做过？

24 Who will not have done? Shéi méiyǒu zuòguò? **谁**没有做过？

25 Who will have done? Shéi huì zuòguò? **谁**会做过？

26 Who will have not done? Shéi hái méiyǒu zuòguò? **谁**还没有做过？

Type 9

1 I can do Wǒ kěyǐ 我可以

2 I can't do wǒ zuò bù dào 我做不到

3 Can I do? wǒ kěbù kěyǐ zuò? 我可不可以做？

4 Can I not do? Wǒ kěyǐ bù zuò ma? 我可以不做**吗**？

5 I can do, can't I? Wǒ kěyǐ, bùshì ma? 我可以，不是**吗**？

6 I can't do, can I? Wǒ zuò bù dào, kěyǐ ma? 我做不到，可以**吗**？

7 What can I do? Wǒ néng zuò shénme? 我能做什么？

8 What can I not do? Wǒ bùnéng zuò shénme? 我不能做什么？

9 Why can I do? Wèishéme wǒ kěyǐ? **为**什么我可以？

10 Why can I not do? Wèishéme wǒ zuò bù dào? **为**什么我做不到？

11 How can I do? Wǒ néng zěnme zuò? 我能怎么做？

12 How can I not do? Wǒ zěnme zuò bù dào? 我怎么做不到？

13 When can I do? Wǒ shénme shíhòu kěyǐ zuò? 我什么时候可以做？

14 When can I not do? Wǒ shénme shíhòu bùnéng zuò? 我什么时候不能做？

15 Where can I do? Wǒ kěyǐ zài nǎlǐ zuò? 我可以在哪里做？

16 Where can I not do? Nǎlǐ bùnéng zuò? 哪里不能做？

17 What can I do for? Wǒ néng zuò shénme? 我能做什么？

18 What can I not do for? Wǒ bùnéng zuò shénme? 我不能做什么？

19 Whom can I do for? Wǒ néng wéi shéi zuò? 我能**为谁**做？

20 Whom can I not do for? Wǒ bùnéng wéi shéi zuò? 我不能**为谁**做？

21 Whom can I do for? Wǒ néng wéi shéi zuò? 我能**为谁**做？

22 Whom can I not do for? Wǒ bùnéng wéi shéi zuò? 我不能**为谁**做？

23 Who can do? Shéi néng zuò dào? 谁能做到？

24 Who can't do? Shéi zuò bù dào? 谁做不到？

25 Who can do? Shéi néng zuò dào? 谁能做到？

26 Who can do? Shéi néng zuò dào? 谁能做到？

Type 10

1 I could do. Wǒ kěyǐ zuò. 我可以做。

2 I could not do. Wǒ zuò bù dào. 我做不到。

3 Could I do? Wǒ kěyǐ ma? 我可以吗？

4 Could I not do? Wǒ kěyǐ bù zuò ma? 我可以不做吗？

5 I could do, couldn't I? Wǒ kěyǐ, bùshì ma? 我可以，不是吗？

6 I could not do, could I? Wǒ zuò bù dào, shì ma? 我做不到，是吗？

7 What could I do? Wǒ néng zuò shénme? 我能做什么？

8 What could I not do? Wǒ bùnéng zuò shénme? 我不能做什么？

9 Why could I do? Wèishéme wǒ kěyǐ? 为什么我可以？

10 Why could I not do? Wèishéme wǒ zuò bù dào? 为什么我做不到？

11 How could I do? Wǒ zěnme bàn? 我怎么办？

12 How could I not do? Wǒ zěnme zuò bù dào? 我怎么做不到？

13 When could I do? Wǒ shénme shíhòu kěyǐ zuò? 我什么时候可以做？

14 When could I not do? Wǒ shénme shíhòu bùnéng zuò? 我什么时候不能做？

15 Where could I do? Wǒ kěyǐ zài nǎlǐ zuò? 我可以在哪里做？

16 Where could I not do? Nǎlǐ bùnéng zuò? 哪里不能做？

17 What could I do for? Wǒ néng zuò shénme? 我能做什么？

18 What could I not do for? Wǒ bùnéng zuò shénme? 我不能做什么？

19 Whom could I do for? Wǒ néng wéi shéi zuò? 我能为谁做？

20 Whom could I not do for? Wǒ bùnéng wéi shéi zuò? 我不能为谁做？

21 Whom could I do with? Wǒ kěyǐ hé shéi yīqǐ zuò? 我可以和谁一起做？

22 Whom could I not do for? Wǒ bùnéng wéi shéi zuò? 我不能为谁做？

23 Who could do? Shéi néng zuò dào? 谁能做到？

24 Who could not do? Shéi zuò bù dào? 谁做不到？

25 Who could not do? Shéi zuò bù dào? 谁做不到？

26 Who could not do? Shéi zuò bù dào? 谁做不到？

Chapter 4

Type 1A. I do. Wǒ zuò. 我做。

1 The Sun rises. Tàiyáng shēng qǐ. 太阳升起。

2 Mother cooks. Māmā zuò fàn. 妈妈做饭。

3 Thief steals at night. Xiǎotōu zài yèjiān tōuqiè. 小偷在夜间偷窃。

4 Father goes to office. Fùqīn qù bàngōngshì. 父亲去办公室。

5 Mr Rabi teaches students. Lā bǐ xiānshēng jiào xuéshēng. 拉比先生教学生。

6 I take light food in the morning. Wǒ zǎoshang chī qīngdàn de shíwù. 我早上吃清淡的食物。

7 The girl comes home at 10 PM at night. Nǚhái wǎnshàng 10 diǎn huí jiā. 女孩晚上10点回家。

8 You sing well. Nǐ chànggē hěn hǎotīng 你唱歌很好听

9 He sees you. tā kànjiàn nǐle. 他看见你了。

10 We eat bread. Wǒmen chī miànbāo. 我们吃面包。

Type 2A. I am doing. Wǒ zài zuò. 我在做。

1 The Sun is rising. Tàiyáng zhèngzài shēng qǐ. 太阳正在升起。

2 Mother is cooking. Māmā zài zuò fàn. 妈妈在做饭。

3 Thief is stealing at night. Xiǎotōu zài yèjiān tōuqiè. 小偷在夜间偷窃。

4 Father is going to office. Fùqīn yào qù bàngōngshì. 父亲要去办公室。

5 Mr Rabi is teaching students. Lā bǐ xiānshēng zhèngzài jiào xuéshēng. 拉比先生正在教学生。

6 I am taking light food in the morning. Wǒ zǎoshang chī qīngdàn de shíwù. 我早上吃清淡的食物。

7 The girl is coming home at 10 PM at night. Nǚhái wǎnshàng 10 diǎn huí jiā. 女孩晚上10点回家。

8 You are singing well. Nǐ chàng dé hěn hǎo. 你唱得很好。

9 He is seeing you. Tā zài jiàn nǐ. 他在见你。

10 We are eating bread. Wǒmen zhèngzài chī miànbāo. 我们正在吃面包。

Type 3A. I have done. Wǒ yǐjīng zuò hǎole. 我已经做好了。

1 The Sun has risen. Tàiyáng yǐjīng shēng qǐ. 太阳已经升起。

2 Mother has cooked. Māmā zhǔ hǎole. 妈妈煮好了。

3 Thief has stolen at night. Xiǎotōu zài wǎnshàng tōule dōngxī. 小偷在晚上偷了东西。

4 Father has gone to office. Fùqīn qù bàngōngshìle. 父亲去办公室了。

5 Mr Rabi has taught students. Lā bǐ xiānshēng jiàoguò xuéshēng. 拉比先生教过学生。

6 I have taken light food in the morning. Wǒ zǎoshang chī qīngdàn de shíwù. 我早上吃清淡的食物。

7 The girl has come home at 10 PM at night. Wǎnshàng 10 diǎn, nǚhái huí jiāle. 晚上10点，女孩回家了。

8 You have sung well. Nǐ chàng dé hěn hǎo. 你唱得很好。

9 He has seen you. Tā jiànguò nǐ. 他见过你。

10 We have eaten bread. Wǒmen chīguò miànbāo. 我们吃过面包。

Type 4A. I did. Wǒ zuò dàole. 我做到了。

1 The Sun rose. Tàiyáng shēng qǐláile. 太阳升起来了。

2 Mother cooked. Māmā zuò fàn. 妈妈做饭。

3 Thief stole at night. Xiǎotōu zài yèjiān tōuqiè. 小偷在夜间偷窃。

4 Father went to office. Fùqīn qù bàngōngshìle. 父亲去办公室了。

5 Mr Rabi taught students. Lā bǐ xiānshēng jiào xuéshēng. 拉比先生教学生。

6 I took light food in the morning. Wǒ zǎoshang chī qīngdàn de shíwù. 我早上吃清淡的食物。

7 The girl came home at 10 PM at night. Wǎnshàng 10 diǎn, nǚhái huí jiāle. 晚上10点，女孩回家了。

8 You sang well. Nǐ chàng dé hěn hǎo. 你唱得很好。

9 He saw you. Tā kànjiàn nǐle. 他看见你了。

10 We ate bread. Wǒmen chīle miànbāo. 我们吃了面包。

Type 5A. I was doing. Wǒ zài zuò. 我在做。

1 The Sun was rising. Tàiyáng zhèngzài shēng qǐ. 太阳正在升起。

2 Mother was cooking. Māmā zhèngzài zuò fàn. 妈妈正在做饭。

3 Thief was stealing at night. Xiǎotōu zài yèjiān tōuqiè. 小偷在夜间偷窃。

4 Father was going to office. Fùqīn yào qù bàngōngshì. 父亲要去办公室。

5 Mr Rabi was teaching students. Lā bǐ xiānshēng zhèngzài jiào xuéshēng. 拉比先生正在教学生。

6 I was taking light food in the morning. Wǒ zǎoshang chī qīngdàn de shíwù. 我早上吃清淡的食物。

7 The girl was coming home at 10 PM at night. Wǎnshàng 10 diǎn, nǚhái cái huí jiā. 晚上10点，女孩才回家。

8 You were singing well. Nǐ chàng dé hěn hǎo. 你唱得很好。

9 He was seeing you. Tā shì lái kàn nǐ de. 他是来看你的。

10 We were eating bread. Wǒmen zhèngzài chī miànbāo. 我们正在吃面包。

Type 6A. I will do. Wǒ huì zuò. 我会做。

1 The Sun will rise. Tàiyáng huì shēng qǐ. 太阳会升起。

2 Mother will cook. Māmā huì zuò fàn. 妈妈会做饭。

3 Thief will steal at night. Xiǎotōu huì zài wǎnshàng tōu dōngxī. 小偷会在晚上偷东西。

4 Father will go to office. Fùqīn jiāng qù bàngōngshì. 父亲将去办公室。

5 Mr Rabi will teach students. Lā bǐ xiānshēng jiāng jiào xuéshēng. 拉比先生将教学生。

6 I will take light food in the morning. Wǒ zǎoshang huì chī qīngdàn de shíwù. 我早上会吃清淡的食物。

7 The girl will come home at 10 PM at night. Nǚhái jiàng zài wǎnshàng 10 diǎn huí jiā. 女孩将在晚上 10 点回家。

8 You will sing well. Nǐ huì chàng dé hěn hǎo. 你会唱得很好。

9 He will see you. Tā huìjiàn dào nǐ de. 他会见到你的。

10 We will eat bread. Wǒmen huì chī miànbāo. 我们会吃面包。

Type 7A.

1 The Sun will be rising. Tàiyáng jiāng shēng qǐ. 太阳将升起。

2 Mother will be cooking. Māmā huì zuò fàn. 妈妈会做饭。

3 Thief will be stealing at night. Xiǎotōu huì zài wǎnshàng tōu dōngxī. 小偷会在晚上偷东西。

4 Father will be going to office. Fùqīn jiāng qù bàngōngshì. 父亲将去办公室。

5 Mr Rabi will be teaching students. Lā bǐ xiānshēng jiāng jiào xuéshēng. 拉比先生将教学生。

6 I will be taking light food in the morning. Wǒ zǎoshang huì chī qīngdàn de shíwù. 我早上会吃清淡的食物。

7 The girl will be coming home at 10 PM at night. Nǚhái jiàng zài wǎnshàng 10 diǎn huí jiā. 女孩将在晚上 10 点回家。

8 You will be singing well. Nǐ huì chàng dé hěn hǎo. 你会唱得很好。

9 He will be seeing you. Tā huì lái kàn nǐ de. 他会来看你的。

10 We will be eating bread. Wǒmen jiāng chī miànbāo. 我们将吃面包。

Type 8A. I will have done. Wǒ huì zuò dào de. 我会做到的。

1 The Sun will have risen. Tàiyáng jiāng shēng qǐ. 太阳将升起。

2 Mother will have cooked. Māmā huì zuò fàn de. 妈妈会做饭的。

3 Thief will have stolen at night. Xiǎotōu huì zài wǎnshàng tōu dōngxī. 小偷会在晚上偷东西。

4 Father will have gone to office. Fùqīn jiāng qù bàngōngshì. 父亲将去办公室。

5 Mr Rabi will have taught students. Lā bǐ xiānshēng huì jiào xuéshēng. 拉比先生会教学生。

6 I will have taken light food in the morning. Wǒ zǎoshang huì chī qīngdàn de shíwù. 我早上会吃清淡的食物。

7 The girl will have come home at 10 PM at night. Nǚhái jiàng zài wǎnshàng 10 diǎn huí jiā. 女孩将在晚上 10 点回家。

8 You will have sung well. Nǐ huì chàng dé hěn hǎo. 你会唱得很好。

9 He will have seen you. Tā huì kàn dào nǐ de. 他会看到你的。

10 We will have eaten bread. Wǒmen huì chī miànbāo de. 我们会吃面包的。

Type 9A. I can do. Wǒ kěyǐ. 我可以。

1 The Sun can rise. Tàiyáng kěyǐ shēng qǐ. 太阳可以升起。

2 Mother can cook. Māmā huì zuò fàn. 妈妈会做饭。

3 Thief can steal at night. Xiǎotōu kěyǐ zài wǎnshàng tōu dōngxī. 小偷可以在晚上偷东西。

4 Father can go to office. Fùqīn kěyǐ qù bàngōngshì. 父亲可以去办公室。

5 Mr Rabi can teach students. Lā bǐ xiānshēng kěyǐ jiào xuéshēng. 拉比先生可以教学生。

6 I can take light food in the morning. Wǒ zǎoshang kěyǐ chī qīngdàn de shíwù. 我早上可以吃清淡的食物。

7 The girl can come home at 10 PM at night. Nǚhái wǎnshàng 10 diǎn kěyǐ huí jiā. 女孩晚上10点可以回家。

8 You can sing well. Nǐ kěyǐ chàng dé hěn hǎo. 你可以唱得很好。

9 He can see you. Tā néng kànjiàn nǐ. 他能看见你。

10 We can eat bread. Wǒmen kěyǐ chī miànbāo. 我们可以吃面包。

Type 10A. I could do. Wǒ kěyǐ zuò. 我可以做。

1 The Sun could rise. Tàiyáng kěyǐ shēng qǐ. 太阳可以升起。

2 Mother could cook. Māmā huì zuò fàn. 妈妈会做饭。

3 Thief could steal at night. Xiǎotōu kěyǐ zài wǎnshàng tōuqiè. 小偷可以在晚上偷窃。

4 Father could go to office. Fùqīn kěyǐ qù bàngōngshì. 父亲可以去办公室。

5 Mr Rabi could teach students. Lā bǐ xiānshēng kěyǐ jiào xuéshēng. 拉比先生可以教学生。

6 I could take light food in the morning. Wǒ zǎoshang kěyǐ chī qīngdàn de shíwù. 我早上可以吃清淡的食物。

7 The girl could come home at 10 PM at night. Nǚhái kěyǐ zài wǎnshàng 10 diǎn huí jiā. 女孩可以在晚上 10 点回家。

8 You could sing well. Nǐ kěyǐ chàng dé hěn hǎo. 你可以唱得很好。

9 He could see you. Tā néng kànjiàn nǐ. 他能看见你。

10 We could eat bread. Wǒmen kěyǐ chī miànbāole. 我们可以吃面包了。

Negative Sentences

Type 1B. I don't do. Wǒ bù zuò. 我不做。

1 The Sun doesn't rise. Tàiyáng méiyǒu shēng qǐ. 太阳没有升起。

2 Mother doesn't cook. Māmā bù zuò fàn. 妈妈不做饭。

3 Thief doesn't steal at night. Xiǎotōu wǎnshàng bù tōu dōngxī. 小偷晚上不偷东西。

4 Father doesn't go to office. Fùqīn bù qù bàngōngshì. 父亲不去办公室。

5 Mr Rabi doesn't teach students. Lā bǐ xiānshēng bù jiào xuéshēng. 拉比先生不教学生。

6 I don't take light food in the morning. Wǒ zǎoshang bù chī qīngdàn de shíwù. 我早上不吃清淡的食物。

7 The girl doesn't come home at 10 PM at night. Nǚhái wǎnshàng 10 diǎn bù huí jiā. 女孩晚上10点不回家。

8 You don't sing well. Nǐ chànggē bù hǎotīng. 你唱歌不好听。

9 He doesn't see you. Tā kàn bùjiàn nǐ. 他看不见你。

10 We don't eat bread. Wǒmen bù chī miànbāo. 我们不吃面包。

Type 2b. I am not doing. Wǒ bùshì zài zuò. 我不是在做。

1 The Sun is not rising. Tàiyáng méiyǒu shēng qǐ. 太阳没有升起。

2 Mother is not cooking. Māmā bù zuò fàn. 妈妈不做饭。

3 Thief is not stealing at night. Xiǎotōu wǎnshàng bù tōu. 小偷晚上不偷。

4 Father is not going to office. Fùqīn bù qù bàngōngshì. 父亲不去办公室。

5 Mr Rabi is not teaching students. Lā bǐ xiānshēng bùshì zài jiào xuéshēng. 拉比先生不是在教学生。

6 I am not taking light food in the morning. Wǒ zǎoshang bù chī qīngdàn de shíwù. 我早上不吃清淡的食物。

7 The girl is not coming home at 10 PM at night. Nǚhái wǎnshàng 10 diǎn bù huí jiā. 女孩晚上10点不回家。

8 You are not singing well. Nǐ chàng dé bù hǎo. 你唱得不好。

9 He is not seeing you. Tā bùjiàn nǐ. 他不见你。

10 We are not eating bread. Wǒmen bù chī miànbāo. 我们不吃面包。

Type 3b. I have not done. Wǒ méiyǒu zuòguò. 我没有做过。

1 The Sun has not risen. Tàiyáng hái méiyǒu shēng qǐ. 太阳还没有升起。

2 Mother has not cooked. Māmā méiyǒu zuò fàn. 妈妈没有做饭。

3 Thief has not stolen at night. Zéi yè wèi tōu. 贼夜未偷。

4 Father has not gone to office. Fùqīn méiyǒu qù bàngōngshì. 父亲没有去办公室。

5 Mr Rabi has not taught students. Lā bǐ xiānshēng méiyǒu jiàoguò xuéshēng. 拉比先生没有教过学生。

6 I have not taken light food in the morning. Wǒ zǎoshang méiyǒu chī qīngdàn de shíwù. 我早上没有吃清淡的食物。

7 The girl has not come home at 10 PM at night. Wǎnshàng 10 diǎn, nǚhái hái méiyǒu huí jiā. 晚上10点，女孩还没有回家。

8 You have not sung well. Nǐ chàng dé bù hǎo. 你唱得不好。

9 He has not seen you. Tā méiyǒu jiànguò nǐ. 他没有见过你。

10 We have not eaten bread. Wǒmen méiyǒu chī miànbāo. 我们没有吃面包。

Type 4b. I did not do. Wǒ méiyǒu zuò. 我没有做。

1 The Sun didn't rise. Tàiyáng méiyǒu shēng qǐ. 太阳没有升起。

2 Mother didn't cook. Māmā méiyǒu zuò fàn. 妈妈没有做饭。

3 Thief didn't steal at night. Xiǎotōu wǎnshàng bù tōu dōngxī. 小偷晚上不偷东西。

4 Father didn't go to office. Fùqīn méiyǒu qù bàngōngshì. 父亲没有去办公室。

5 Mr Rabi didn't teach students. Lā bǐ xiānshēng méiyǒu jiào xuéshēng. 拉比先生没有教学生。

6 I didn't take light food in the morning. Wǒ zǎoshang méiyǒu chī qīngdàn de shíwù. 我早上没有吃清淡的食物。

7 The girl didn't come home 10 PM at night. Wǎnshàng 10 diǎn, nǚhái méiyǒu huí jiā. 晚上10点，女孩没有回家。

8 You didn't sing well. Nǐ chàng dé bù hǎo. 你唱得不好。

9 He didn't see you. Tā méi kànjiàn nǐ. 他没看见你。

10 We didn't eat bread. Wǒmen méiyǒu chī miànbāo. 我们没有吃面包。

Type 5b. I was not doing. Wǒ bùshì zài zuò. 我不是在做。

1 The Sun was not rising. Tàiyáng méiyǒu shēng qǐ. 太阳没有升起。

2 Mother was not cooking. Māmā méiyǒu zuò fàn. 妈妈没有做饭。

3 Thief was not stealing at night. Xiǎotōu wǎnshàng bù tōu dōngxī. 小偷晚上不偷东西。

4 Father was not going to office. Fùqīn bù qù bàngōngshì. 父亲不去办公室。

5 Mr Rabi was not teaching students. Lā bǐ xiānshēng méiyǒu jiào xuéshēng. 拉比先生没有教学生。

6 I was not taking light food in the morning. Wǒ zǎoshang méiyǒu chī qīngdàn de shíwù. 我早上没有吃清淡的食物。

7 The girl was not coming home at 10 PM at night. Wǎnshàng 10 diǎn, nǚhái hái méiyǒu huí jiā. 晚上10点，女孩还没有回家。

8 You were not singing well. Nǐ chàng dé bù hǎo. 你唱得不好。

9 He was not seeing you. Tā méiyǒu kàn dào nǐ. 他没有看到你。

10 We were not eating bread. Wǒmen méiyǒu chī miànbāo. 我们没有吃面包。

Type 6b. I will not do. Wǒ bù huì. 我不会。

1 The Sun will not rise. Tàiyáng bù huì shēng qǐ. 太阳不会升起。

2 Mother will not cook. Māmā bù huì zuò fàn. 妈妈不会做饭。

3 Thief will not steal at night. Xiǎotōu wǎnshàng bù huì tōu dōngxī. 小偷晚上不会偷东西。

4 Father will not go to office. Fùqīn bù huì qù bàngōngshì. 父亲不会去办公室。

5 Mr Rabi will not teach students. Lā bǐ xiānshēng bù huì jiào xuéshēng. 拉比先生不会教学生。

6 I will not take light food in the morning. Wǒ zǎoshang bù huì chī qīngdàn de shíwù. 我早上不会吃清淡的食物。

7 The girl will not come home at 10 PM at night. Nǚhái wǎnshàng 10 diǎn bù huí jiā. 女孩晚上10点不回家。

8 You will not sing well. Nǐ bù huì chàng dé hǎo. 你不会唱得好。

9 He will not see you. Tā bù huìjiàn nǐ. 他不会见你。

10 We will not eat bread. Wǒmen bù huì chī miànbāo. 我们不会吃面包。

Type 7b. I will be doing. Wǒ huì zuò de. 我会做的。

1 The Sun will be rising. Tàiyáng jiāng shēng qǐ. 太阳将升起。

2 Mother will be cooking. Māmā huì zuò fàn. 妈妈会做饭。

3 Thief will be stealing at night. Xiǎotōu huì zài wǎnshàng tōu dōngxī. 小偷会在晚上偷东西。

4 Father will be going to office. Fùqīn jiāng qù bàngōngshì. 父亲将去办公室。

5 Mr Rabi will be teaching students. Lā bǐ xiānshēng jiāng jiào xuéshēng. 拉比先生将教学生。

6 I will be taking light food in the morning. Wǒ zǎoshang huì chī qīngdàn de shíwù. 我早上会吃清淡的食物。

7 The girl will not be coming home at 10 PM at night. Nǚhái wǎnshàng 10 diǎn bù huì huí jiā. 女孩晚上10点不会回家。

8 You will not be singing well. Nǐ bù huì chàng dé hěn hǎo. 你不会唱得很好。

9 He will not be seeing you. Tā bù huìjiàn nǐ de. 他不会见你的。

10 We will not be eating bread. Wǒmen bù huì chī miànbāo. 我们不会吃面包。

Type 8b. I will not have done. Wǒ bù huì zuò de. 我不会做的。

1 The Sun will not have risen. Tàiyáng bù huì shēng qǐ. 太阳不会升起。

2 Mother will not have cooked. Māmā bù huì zuò fàn. 妈妈不会做饭。

3 Thief will not have stolen at night. Xiǎotōu wǎnshàng bù huì tōu de. 小偷晚上不会偷的。

4 Father will not have gone to office. Fùqīn bù huì qù bàngōngshì. 父亲不会去办公室。

5 Mr Rabi will not have taught students. Lā bǐ xiānshēng bù huì jiào xuéshēng. 拉比先生不会教学生。

6 I will not have taken light food in the morning. Wǒ zǎoshang bù huì chī qīngdàn de shíwù. 我早上不会吃清淡的食物。

7 The girl will not have come home at 10 PM at night. Nàgè nǚhái wǎnshàng 10 diǎn bù huì huí jiā. 那个女孩晚上 10 点不会回家。

8 You will not have sung well. Nǐ bù huì chàng dé hǎo. 你不会唱得好。

9 He will not have seen you. Tā bù huì kànjiàn nǐ de. 他不会看见你的。

10 We will not have eaten bread. Wǒmen bù huì chī miànbāo. 我们不会吃面包。

Type 9b. I can not do. Wǒ bùnéng zuò. 我不能做。

1 The Sun can not rise. Tàiyáng shēng bù qǐlái. 太阳升不起来。

2 Mother can not cook. Māmā bù huì zuò fàn. 妈妈不会做饭。

3 Thief can not steal at night. Xiǎotōu wǎnshàng bùnéng tōu. 小偷晚上不能偷。

4 Father can not go to office. Fùqīn bùnéng qù bàngōngshì. 父亲不能去办公室。

5 Mr Rabi can not teach students. Lā bǐ xiānshēng bùnéng jiào xuéshēng. 拉比先生不能教学生。

6 I can not take light food in the morning. Wǒ zǎoshang bùnéng chī qīngdàn de shíwù. 我早上不能吃清淡的食物。

7 The girl can not come home at 10 PM at night. Nǚhái wǎnshàng 10 diǎn bùnéng huí jiā. 女孩晚上10点不能回家。

8 You can not sing well. Nǐ bùnéng chàng dé hǎo. 你不能唱得好。

9 He can not see you. Tā kàn bùjiàn nǐ. 他看不见你。

10 We can not eat bread. Wǒmen bùnéng chī miànbāo. 我们不能吃面包。

Type 10b. I could not do. Wǒ zuò bù dào. 我做不到。

1 The Sun could not rise. Tàiyáng wúfǎ shēng qǐ. 太阳无法升起。

2 Mother could not cook. Māmā bù huì zuò fàn. 妈妈不会做饭。

3 Thief could not steal at night. Xiǎotōu wǎnshàng bùnéng tōu dōngxī. 小偷晚上不能偷东西。

4 Father could not go to office. Fùqīn bùnéng qù bàngōngshì. 父亲不能去办公室。

5 Mr Rabi could not teach students. Lā bǐ xiānshēng wúfǎ jiào xuéshēng. 拉比先生无法教学生。

6 I could not take light food in the morning. Wǒ zǎoshang bùnéng chī qīngdàn de shíwù. 我早上不能吃清淡的食物。

7 The girl could not come home at 10 PM at night. Wǎnshàng 10 diǎn, nǚhái wúfǎ huí jiā. 晚上10点，女孩无法回家。

8 You could not sing well. Nǐ chàng dé bù hǎo. 你唱得不好。

9 He could not see you. Tā kàn bùjiàn nǐ. 他看不见你。

10 We could not eat bread. Wǒmen bùnéng chī miànbāo. 我们不能吃面包。

Type 1C. Do I do? Wǒ zuò ma? 我做吗？

1 Does the Sun rise? Tàiyáng shēng qǐláile ma? 太阳升起来了吗？

2 Does mother cook? Māmā zuò fàn ma? 妈妈做饭吗？

3 Does thief steal at night? Xiǎotōu wǎnshàng tōu dōngxī ma? 小偷晚上偷东西吗？

4 Does Father go to office? Bàba qù bàngōngshì ma? 爸爸去办公室吗？

5 Does Mr Rabi teach students? Lā bǐ xiānshēng jiào xuéshēng ma? 拉比先生教学生**吗**？

6 Do I take p'light food in the morning? Wǒ zǎoshang chī qīng shí ma? 我早上吃**轻**食**吗**？

7 Does the girl come home at 10 PM at night? Nǚhái wǎnshàng 10 diǎn huí jiā ma? 女孩晚上10点回家**吗**？

8 Do you sing well? Nǐ chànggē hǎo ma? 你唱歌好**吗**？

9 Does he see you? Tā kànjiàn nǐle ma? 他看见你了**吗**？

10 Do we eat bread? Wǒmen chī miànbāo ma? 我**们**吃面包**吗**？

Type 2C Am I doing ? Wǒ zài zuò shénme? 我在做什么？

1 Is the Sun rising ? Tàiyáng shēng qǐláile ma? 太阳升起来了**吗**？

2 Is mother cooking ? Māmā zài zuò fàn ma? **妈妈**在做**饭吗**？

3 Is thief stealing at night ? Xiǎotōu wǎnshàng tōu dōngxī ma? 小偷晚上偷东西**吗**？

4 Is father going to office ? Bàba yào qù shàngbān ma? 爸爸要去上班**吗**？

5 Is Mr Rabi teaching students ? Lā bǐ xiānshēng zài jiào xuéshēng ma? 拉比先生在教学生**吗**？

6 AM I taking light food in the morning ? Wǒ zǎoshang chī qīngdàn de shíwù ma? 我早上吃清淡的食物**吗**？

7 Is the girl coming home at 10 PM at night ? Nǚhái wǎnshàng 10 diǎn huí jiā ma? 女孩晚上10点回家**吗**？

8 Are you singing well ? Nǐ chàng dé hǎo ma? 你唱得好**吗**？

9 Is he seeing you ? Tā zài jiàn nǐ ma? 他在见你**吗**？

10 Are we are eating bread ? Wǒmen zài chī miànbāo ma? 我**们**在吃面包**吗**？

Type 3C. Have I done ? Wǒ zuòle ma? 我做了**吗**？

1 Has The Sun risen ? Tàiyáng shēng qǐláile ma? 太阳升起来了**吗**？

2 Has mother cooked ? Māmā zuò fànle ma? **妈妈**做**饭**了**吗**？

3 Has thief stolen at night ? Xiǎotōu yèjiān tōuqièle ma? 小偷夜间偷窃了**吗**？

4 Has father gone to office ? Bàba qù bàngōngshìle ma? 爸爸去办公室了**吗**？

5 Has Mr Rabi taught students ? Lā bǐ xiānshēng jiàoguò xuéshēng ma? 拉比先生教过学生**吗**？

6 Have I taken light food in the morning ? Wǒ zǎoshang chī qīngdàn de shíwùle ma? 我早上吃清淡的食物了**吗**？

7 Has the girl come home at 10 PM at night ? Nǚhái wǎnshàng 10 diǎn huí jiāle ma? 女孩晚上10点回家了**吗**？

8 Have You sung well ? Nǐ chàng dé hǎo ma? 你唱得好**吗**？

9 Has he seen you ? Tā jiànguò nǐ ma? 他见过你**吗**？

10 Have We eaten bread ? Wǒmen chīguò miànbāo ma? 我**们**吃过面包**吗**？

Type 4C. Did I do? Wǒ zuòle ma? 我做了**吗**？

1 Did the Sun rise? Tàiyáng shēng qǐláile ma? 太阳升起来了**吗**？

2 Did mother cook? Māmā zuò fànle ma? **妈妈**做**饭**了**吗**？

3 Did thief steal at night? Xiǎotōu wǎnshàng tōu dōngxī ma? 小偷晚上偷东西**吗**？

4 Did father go to office? Bàba qù bàngōngshìle ma? 爸爸去办公室了**吗**？

5 Did Mr Rabi teach students? Lā bǐ xiānshēng jiàoguò xuéshēng ma? 拉比先生教过学生**吗**？

6 Did I take light food in the morning? Wǒ zǎoshang chī qīngdàn de shíwùle ma? 我早上吃清淡的食物了**吗**？

7 Did the girl come home at 10 PM at night? Nà nǚhái wǎnshàng 10 diǎn cái huí jiā ma? 那女孩晚上10点才回家**吗**？

8 Did you sing well? Nǐ chàng dé hǎo ma? 你唱得好**吗**？

9 Did he see you? Tā kàn dào nǐle ma? 他看到你了**吗**？

10 Did we eat bread? Wǒmen chī miànbāole ma? 我**们**吃面包了**吗**？

Type 5C. Was I doing? Wǒ zài zuò shénme? 我在做什么？

1 Was the Sun rising? Tàiyáng shēng qǐle ma? 太阳升起了**吗**？

2 Was mother cooking? Māmā zài zuò fàn ma? **妈妈**在做**饭吗**？

3 Was thief stealing at night? Xiǎotōu zài yèjiān tōuqiè ma? 小偷在夜间偷窃**吗**？

4 Was father going to office? Bàba yào qù bàngōngshì ma? 爸爸要去办公室**吗**？

5 Was Mr Rabi teaching students? Lā bǐ xiānshēng zài jiào xuéshēng ma? 拉比先生在教学生**吗**？

6 Was I taking light food in the morning? Wǒ zǎoshang chī qīngdàn de shíwù ma? 我早上吃清淡的食物**吗**？

7 Was the girl coming home at 10 PM at night? Nǚhái wǎnshàng 10 diǎn huí jiā ma? 女孩晚上10点回家**吗**？

8 Were you singing well? Nǐ chàng dé hǎo ma? 你唱得好**吗**？

9 Was he seeing you? Tā jiànguò nǐ ma? 他见过你**吗**？

10 Were we eating bread? Wǒmen chī miànbāole ma? 我们吃面包了**吗**？

Type 6C. Will I do? Wǒ huì zuò ma? 我会做**吗**？

1 Will the Sun rise? Tàiyáng huì shēng qǐ ma? 太阳会升起**吗**？

2 Will Mother cook? Māmā huì zuò fàn ma? **妈妈**会做**饭吗**？

3 Will thief steal at night? Xiǎotōu wǎnshàng huì tōu dōngxī ma? 小偷晚上会偷东西**吗**？

4 Will father go to office? Bàba huì qù bàngōngshì ma? 爸爸会去办公室**吗**？

5 Will Mr Rabi teach students? Lā bǐ xiānshēng huì jiào xuéshēng ma? 拉比先生会教学生**吗**？

6 Will I take light food in the morning? Wǒ zǎoshang huì chī qīngdàn de shíwù ma? 我早上会吃清淡的食物**吗**？

7 Will the girl come home at 10 PM at night? Nǚhái wǎnshàng 10 diǎn huì huí jiā ma? 女孩晚上10点会回家**吗**？

8 Will you sing well? Nǐ huì chànggē ma? 你会唱歌**吗**？

9 Will he see you? Tā huìjiàn nǐ ma? 他会见你**吗**？

10 Will we eat bread? Wǒmen huì chī miànbāo ma? 我们会吃面包**吗**？

Type 7C. Will I be doing? Wǒ huì zuò ma? 我会做**吗**？

1 Will the Sun be rising? Tàiyáng huì shēng qǐ ma? 太阳会升起**吗**？

2 Will mother be cooking? Māmā huì zuò fàn ma? **妈妈**会做**饭吗**？

3 Will thief be stealing at night? Xiǎotōu huì zài wǎnshàng tōu dōngxī ma? 小偷会在晚上偷东西**吗**？

4 Will father be going to office? Bàba huì qù bàngōngshì ma? 爸爸会去办公室**吗**？

5 Will Mr Rabi be teaching students? Lā bǐ xiānshēng huì jiào xuéshēng ma? 拉比先生会教学生**吗**？

6 Will I be taking light food in the morning? Wǒ zǎoshang huì chī qīngdàn de shíwù ma? 我早上会吃清淡的食物**吗**？

7 Will the girl be coming home at 10 PM at night? Nǚhái wǎnshàng 10 diǎn huì huí jiā ma? 女孩晚上10点会回家**吗**？

8 Will you be singing well? Nǐ huì chànggē hǎo ma? 你会唱歌好**吗**？

9 Will he be seeing you? Tā huì lái kàn nǐ ma? 他会来看你吗？

10 Will we be eating bread? Wǒmen huì chī miànbāo ma? 我们会吃面包吗？

Type 8C. Will I have done? Wǒ huì zuò ma? 我会做吗？

1 Will the Sun have risen? Tàiyáng huì shēng qǐ ma? 太阳会升起吗？

2 Will mother have cooked? Māmā huì zuò fàn ma? 妈妈会做饭吗？

3 Will thief have stolen at night? Xiǎotōu huì zài wǎnshàng tōu dōngxī ma? 小偷会在晚上偷东西吗？

4 Will father have gone to office? Fùqīn huì qù bàngōngshì ma? 父亲会去办公室吗？

5 Will Mr Rabi have taught students? Lā bǐ xiānshēng huì jiào xuéshēng ma? 拉比先生会教学生吗？

6 Will I have taken light food in the morning? Wǒ zǎoshang huì chī qīngdàn de shíwù ma? 我早上会吃清淡的食物吗？

7 Will the girl have come home at 10 PM at night? Nǚhái wǎnshàng 10 diǎn huì huí jiā ma? 女孩晚上10点会回家吗？

8 Will you have sung well? Nǐ huì chàng dé hǎo ma? 你会唱得好吗？

9 Will he have seen you? Tā huì kànjiàn nǐ ma? 他会看见你吗？

10 Will we have eaten bread? Wǒmen huì chī miànbāo ma? 我们会吃面包吗？

Type 9C. Can I do? Wǒ kěbù kěyǐ zuò? 我可不可以做？

1 Can the Sun rise? Tàiyángnéng shēng qǐ ma? 太阳能升起吗？

2 Can mother cook? Māmā huì zuò fàn ma? 妈妈会做饭吗？

3 Can thief steal at night? Xiǎotōu wǎnshàng néng tōu dōngxī ma? 小偷晚上能偷东西吗？

4 Can father go to office? Bàba kěyǐ qù bàngōngshì ma? 爸爸可以去办公室吗？

5 Can Mr Rabi teach students? Lā bǐ xiānshēng kěyǐ jiào xuéshēng ma? 拉比先生可以教学生吗？

6 Can I take light food in the morning? Zǎoshang kěyǐ chī qīngdàn de shíwù ma? 早上可以吃清淡的食物吗？

7 Can the girl come home at 10 PM at night? Nǚhái wǎnshàng 10 diǎn kěyǐ huí jiā ma? 女孩晚上10点可以回家吗？

8 Can you sing well? Nǐ huì chànggē ma? 你会唱歌吗？

9 Can he see you? Tā néng kànjiàn nǐ ma? 他能看见你吗？

10 Can we eat bread? Wǒmen kěyǐ chī miànbāo ma? 我们可以吃面包吗？

Type 10C. Could I do? Wǒ kěyǐ ma? 我可以吗？

1 Could the Sun rise? Tàiyángnéng shēng qǐ ma? 太阳能升起吗？

2 Could mother cook? Māmā huì zuò fàn ma? 妈妈会做饭吗？

3 Could thief steal at night? Xiǎotōu wǎnshàng huì tōu dōngxī ma? 小偷晚上会偷东西吗？

4 Could father go to office? Bàba kěyǐ qù bàngōngshì ma? 爸爸可以去办公室吗？

5 Could Mr Rabi teach students? Lā bǐ xiānshēng kěyǐ jiào xuéshēng ma? 拉比先生可以教学生吗？

6 Could I take light food in the morning? Zǎoshang kěyǐ chī qīngdàn de shíwù ma? 早上可以吃清淡的食物吗？

7 Could the girl come home at 10 PM at night? Nǚhái wǎnshàng 10 diǎn néng huí jiā ma? 女孩晚上10点能回家吗？

8 Could you sing well? Nǐ huì chànggē ma? 你会唱歌吗？

9 Could he see you? Tā néng jiàn dào nǐ ma? 他能见到你吗？

10 Could we eat bread? Wǒmen kěyǐ chī miànbāo ma? 我们可以吃面包吗？

Type 1D. Do I not do? Wǒ bù zuò ma? 我不做吗？

1 Does the Sun not rise? Tàiyáng bù shēng qǐ ma? 太阳不升起吗？

2 Does mother not cook? Māmā bù zuò fàn? 妈妈不做饭？

3 Does thief not steal at night? Xiǎotōu wǎnshàng bù tōu dōngxī ma? 小偷晚上不偷东西吗？

4 Does Father not go to office? Bàba bù qù bàngōngshì ma? 爸爸不去办公室吗？

5 Does Mr Rabi not teach students? Lā bǐ xiānshēng bù jiào xuéshēng ma? 拉比先生不教学生吗？

6 Do I not take light food in the morning? Wǒ zǎoshang bù chī qīngdàn de shíwù ma? 我早上不吃清淡的食物吗？

7 Does the girl not come home at 10 PM at night? Nǚhái wǎnshàng 10 diǎn bù huí jiā ma? 女孩晚上10点不回家吗？

8 Do you not sing well? Nǐ chànggē bù hǎotīng ma? 你唱歌不好听吗？

9 Does he not see you? Tā kàn bùjiàn nǐ ma? 他看不见你吗？

10 Do we not eat bread? Wǒmen bù chī miànbāo ma? 我们不吃面包吗？

Type 2D. Am I not doing ? Wǒ bùshì zài zuò ma? 我不是在做吗？

1 Is the Sun not rising ? Tàiyáng méiyǒu shēng qǐ ma? 太阳没有升起吗？

2 Is mother not cooking ? Māmā bù zuò fàn ma? 妈妈不做饭吗？

3 Is thief not stealing at night ? Xiǎotōu bùshì wǎnshàng tōu de ma? 小偷不是晚上偷的吗？

4 Is father not going to office ? Bàba bù qù shàngbān ma? 爸爸不去上班吗？

5 Is Mr Rabi not teaching students ? Lā bǐ xiānshēng bùshì zài jiào xuéshēng ma? 拉比先生不是在教学生吗？

6 AM I not taking light food in the morning ? Wǒ zǎoshang bù chī qīngdàn de shíwù ma? 我早上不吃清淡的食物吗？

7 Is the girl not coming home at 10 PM at night ? Nǚhái wǎnshàng 10 diǎn bù huí jiā ma? 女孩晚上10点不回家吗？

8 Are you not singing well ? Nǐ chànggē bù hǎotīng ma? 你唱歌不好听吗？

9 Is he not seeing you ? Tā méi jiàn nǐ ma? 他没见你吗？

10 Are we not eating bread ? Wǒmen bùshì zài chī miànbāo ma? 我们不是在吃面包吗？

Type 3D. Have I not done ? Wǒ méiyǒu zuòguò ma? 我没有做过吗？

1 Has The Sun not risen ? Tàiyáng hái méi shēng qǐ? 太阳还没升起？

2 Has mother not cooked ? Māmā méi zuò fàn ma? 妈妈没做饭吗？

3 Has thief not stolen at night? Xiǎotōu bùshì wǎnshàng tōu de ma? 小偷不是晚上偷的吗？

4 Has father not gone to office? Bàba méi qù bàngōngshì ma? 爸爸没去办公室吗？

5 Has Mr Rabi not taught students? Lā bǐ xiānshēng méiyǒu jiàoguò xuéshēng ma? 拉比先生没有教过学生吗？

6 Have I not taken light food in the morning ? Wǒ zǎoshang méiyǒu chī qīngdàn de shíwù ma? 我早上没有吃清淡的食物吗？

7 Has the girl not come home at 10 PM at night ? Nǚhái wǎnshàng 10 diǎn méi huí jiā ma? 女孩晚上10点没回家吗？

8 Have You not sung well ? Nǐ chàng dé bù hǎo ma? 你唱得不好吗？

9 Has he not seen you ? Tā méi jiànguò nǐ ma? 他没见过你吗？

10 Have We not eaten bread? Wǒmen méiyǒu chīguò miànbāo ma? 我们没有吃过面包吗？

Type 4D. Did I not do? Wǒ méiyǒu zuò ma? 我没有做吗？

1 Did the Sun not rise? Tàiyáng méiyǒu shēng qǐ ma? 太阳没有升起吗？

2 Did mother not cook? Māmā méiyǒu zuò fàn ma? 妈妈没有做饭吗？

3 Did thief not steal at night? Xiǎotōu bùshì wǎnshàng tōu de ma? 小偷不是晚上偷的吗？

4 Did father not go to office? Bàba méi qù bàngōngshì ma? 爸爸没去办公室吗？

5 Did Mr Rabi not teach students? Lā bǐ xiānshēng méiyǒu jiào xuéshēng ma? 拉比先生没有教学生吗？

6 Did I not take light food in the morning? Wǒ zǎoshang méiyǒu chī qīngdàn de shíwù ma? 我早上没有吃清淡的食物吗？

7 Did the girl not come home at 10 PM at night? Gūniáng wǎnshàng 10 diǎn méi huí jiā ma? 姑娘晚上10点没回家吗？

8 Did you not sing well? Nǐ chàng dé bù hǎo ma? 你唱得不好吗？

9 Did he not see you? Tā méi kànjiàn nǐ ma? 他没看见你吗？

10 Did we not eat bread? Wǒmen méi chī miànbāo ma? 我们没吃面包吗？

Type 5D. Was I not doing? Wǒ bùshì zài zuò ma? 我不是在做吗？

1 Was the Sun not rising? Tàiyáng méiyǒu shēng qǐ ma? 太阳没有升起吗？

2 Was mother not cooking? Māmā bù zuò fàn ma? 妈妈不做饭吗？

3 Was thief not stealing at night? Xiǎotōu bùshì wǎnshàng tōu de ma? 小偷不是晚上偷的吗？

4 Was father not going to office? Bàba bù qù shàngbān ma? 爸爸不去上班吗？

5 Was Mr Rabi not teaching students? Lā bǐ xiānshēng bùshì zài jiào xuéshēng ma? 拉比先生不是在教学生吗？

6 Was I not taking light food in the morning? Wǒ zǎoshang méiyǒu chī qīngdàn de shíwù ma? 我早上没有吃清淡的食物吗？

7 Was the girl not coming home at 10 PM at night? Nǚhái wǎnshàng 10 diǎn bù huí jiā ma? 女孩晚上10点不回家吗？

8 Were you not singing well? Nǐ chànggē bù hǎotīng ma? 你唱歌不好听吗？

9 Was he not seeing you? Tā méi jiàn nǐ ma? 他没见你吗？

10 Were we not eating bread? Wǒmen bùshì zài chī miànbāo ma? 我们不是在吃面包吗？

Type 6D. Will I not do? Wǒ bù huì ma? 我不会吗？

1 Will the Sun not rise? Tàiyáng bù huì shēng qǐ ma? 太阳不会升起吗？

2 Will Mother not cook? Māmā bù huì zuò fàn ma? 妈妈不会做饭吗？

3 Will thief not steal at night? Xiǎotōu wǎnshàng bù huì tōu dōngxī ma? 小偷晚上不会偷东西吗？

4 Will father not go to office? Bàba bù huì qù bàngōngshì ma? 爸爸不会去办公室吗？

5 Will Mr Rabi not teach students? Lā bǐ xiānshēng bù huì jiào xuéshēng ma? 拉比先生不会教学生吗？

6 Will I not take light food in the morning? Wǒ zǎoshang bù huì chī qīngdàn de shíwù ma? 我早上不会吃清淡的食物吗？

7 Will the girl not come home at 10 PM at night? Nǚhái wǎnshàng 10 diǎn bù huí jiā ma? 女孩晚上10点不回家吗？

8 Will you not sing well? Nǐ bù huì chànggē hǎo ma? 你不会唱歌好吗？

9 Will he not see you? Tā bù huìjiàn nǐ ma? 他不会见你吗？

10 Will we not eat bread? Wǒmen bù chī miànbāo ma? 我们不吃面包吗？

Type 7D. Will I not be doing? Wǒ bù huì zuò ma? 我不会做吗？

1 Will the Sun not be rising? Tàiyáng bù huì shēng qǐ ma? 太阳不会升起吗？

2 Will mother not be cooking? Māmā bù huì zuò fàn ma? 妈妈不会做饭吗？

3 Will thief not be stealing at night? Xiǎotōu wǎnshàng bù huì tōu dōngxī ma? 小偷晚上不会偷东西吗？

4 Will father not be going to office? Bàba bù huì qù bàngōngshì ma? 爸爸不会去办公室吗？

5 Will Mr Rabi not be teaching students? Lā bǐ xiānshēng bù huì jiào xuéshēng ma? 拉比先生不会教学生吗？

6 Will I not be taking light food in the morning? Wǒ zǎoshang bù huì chī qīngdàn de shíwù ma? 我早上不会吃清淡的食物吗？

7 Will the girl not be coming home at 10 PM at night? Nǚhái wǎnshàng 10 diǎn bù huí jiā ma? 女孩晚上10点不回家吗？

8 Will you not be singing well? Nǐ bù huì chànggē hǎo ma? 你不会唱歌好吗？

9 Will he not be seeing you? Tā bù huìjiàn nǐ ma? 他不会见你吗？

10 Will we not be eating bread? Wǒmen bù huì chī miànbāo ma? 我们不会吃面包吗？

Type 8D. Will I not have done? Wǒ bù huì zuò ma? 我不会做吗？

1 Will the Sun not have risen? Tàiyáng bù huì shēng qǐ ma? 太阳不会升起吗？

2 Will mother not have cooked? Māmā bù huì zuò fàn ma? 妈妈不会做饭吗？

3 Will thief not have stolen at night? Xiǎotōu wǎnshàng bù huì tōu dōngxī ma? 小偷晚上不会偷东西吗？

4 Will father not have gone to office? Fùqīn bù huì qù bàngōngshì ma? 父亲不会去办公室吗？

5 Will Mr Rabi not have taught students? Lā bǐ xiānshēng bù huì jiào xuéshēng ma? 拉比先生不会教学生吗？

6 Will I not have taken light food in the morning? Wǒ zǎoshang bù huì chī qīngdàn de shíwù ma? 我早上不会吃清淡的食物吗？

7 Will the girl not have come home at 10 PM at night? Nǚhái wǎnshàng 10 diǎn bù huí jiā ma? 女孩晚上10点不回家吗？

8 Will you not have sung well? Nǐ bù huì chàng dé hěn hǎo ma? 你不会唱得很好吗？

9 Will he not have seen you? Tā bù huìjiànguò nǐ ma? 他不会见过你吗？

10 Will we not have eaten bread? Wǒmen bù huì chī miànbāo ma? 我们不会吃面包吗？

Type 9D. Can I not do? Wǒ kěyǐ bù zuò ma? 我可以不做吗？

1 Can the Sun not rise? Tàiyáng bùnéng shēng qǐ ma? 太阳不能升起吗？

2 Can mother not cook? Māmā bù huì zuò fàn ma? 妈妈不会做饭吗？

3 Can thief not steal at night? Xiǎotōu wǎnshàng bùnéng tōu dōngxī ma? 小偷晚上不能偷东西吗？

4 Can father not go to office? Bàba kěyǐ bù qù bàngōngshì ma? 爸爸可以不去办公室吗？

5 Can Mr Rabi not teach students? Lā bǐ xiānshēng bùnéng jiào xuéshēng ma? 拉比先生不能教学生吗？

6 Can I not take light food in the morning? Zǎoshang bùnéng chī qīngdàn de shíwù ma? 早上不能吃清淡的食物吗？

7 Can the girl not come home at 10 PM at night? Nǚhái wǎnshàng 10 diǎn bùnéng huí jiā ma? 女孩晚上10点不能回家吗？

8 Can you not sing well? Nǐ chànggē bù hǎotīng ma? 你唱歌不好听**吗**？

9 Can he not see you? Tā kàn bùjiàn nǐ ma? 他看不见你**吗**？

10 Can we not eat bread? Wǒmen bùnéng chī miànbāo ma? 我们不能吃面包**吗**？

Type 10D. Could I not do? Wǒ kěyǐ bù zuò ma? 我可以不做**吗**？

1 Could the Sun not rise? Tàiyáng bùnéng shēng qǐ ma? 太阳不能升起**吗**？

2 Could mother not cook? Māmā bù huì zuò fàn ma? 妈妈不会做饭**吗**？

3 Could thief not steal at night? Xiǎotōu wǎnshàng bùnéng tōu dōngxī ma? 小偷晚上不能偷东西**吗**？

4 Could father not go to office? Bàba bùnéng qù bàngōngshì ma? 爸爸不能去办公室**吗**？

5 Could Mr Rabi not teach students? Lā bǐ xiānshēng bùnéng jiào xuéshēng ma? 拉比先生不能教学生**吗**？

6 Could I not take light food in the morning? Zǎoshang bùnéng chī qīngdàn de shíwù ma? 早上不能吃清淡的食物**吗**？

7 Could the girl not come home at 10 PM at night? Nǚhái wǎnshàng 10 diǎn bù huí jiā ma? 女孩晚上10点不回家**吗**？

8 Could you not sing well? Nǐ chànggē bù hǎotīng ma? 你唱歌不好听**吗**？

9 Could he not see you? Tā bùnéng jiàn nǐ ma? 他不能见你**吗**？

10 Could we not eat bread? Wǒmen bùnéng chī miànbāo ma? 我们不能吃面包**吗**？

Type 1E. I do, don't I? Wǒ zuò, bùshì ma? 我做，不是**吗**？

1 The Sun rises, doesn't it? Tàiyáng shēng qǐláile, bùshì ma? 太阳升起来了，不是**吗**？

2 Mother cooks, doesn't she? Māmā zuò fàn, bùshì ma? 妈妈做饭，不是**吗**？

3 Thief steals at night, doesn't he? Xiǎotōu wǎnshàng tōu dōngxī, bùshì ma? 小偷晚上偷东西，不是**吗**？

4 Father goes to office, doesn't he? Fùqīn qù bàngōngshì, shì ma? 父亲去办公室，是**吗**？

5 Mr Rabi teaches students, doesn't he? Lā bǐ xiānshēng jiào xuéshēng, bùshì ma? 拉比先生教学生，不是**吗**？

6 I take light food in the morning, don't I? Wǒ zǎoshang chī qīngdàn de shíwù, bùshì ma? 我早上吃清淡的食物，不是**吗**？

7 The girl comes home at 10 PM at night, doesn't she? Nàgè nǚhái wǎnshàng 10 diǎn huí jiā, shì ma? 那个女孩晚上 10 点回家，是吗？

8 You sing well, don't you? Nǐ chàng dé hěn hǎo, bùshì ma? 你唱得很好，不是吗？

9 He sees you, doesn't he? Tā kàn dào nǐle, bùshì ma? 他看到你了，不是吗？

10 We eat bread, don't we? Wǒmen chī miànbāo, bùshì ma? 我们吃面包，不是吗？

Type 2E. I am doing, am not I? Wǒ zài zuò, bùshì ma? 我在做，不是吗？

1 The Sun is rising, isn't it? Tàiyáng zhèngzài shēng qǐ, bùshì ma? 太阳正在升起，不是吗？

2 Mother is cooking, isn't she? Māmā zài zuò fàn, shì ma? 妈妈在做饭，是吗？

3 Thief is stealing at night, isn't he? Xiǎotōu zài wǎnshàng tōu dōngxī, bùshì ma? 小偷在晚上偷东西，不是吗？

4 Father is going to office, isn't he? Fùqīn yào qù bàngōngshì, shì ma? 父亲要去办公室，是吗？

5 Mr Rabi is teaching students, isn't he? Lā bǐ xiānshēng zhèngzài jiào xuéshēng, shì ma? 拉比先生正在教学生，是吗？

6 I am taking light food in the morning, am not I? Wǒ zǎoshang chī qīngdàn de shíwù, bùshì ma? 我早上吃清淡的食物，不是吗？

7 The girl is coming home at 10 PM at night, isn't she? Nǚhái wǎnshàng 10 diǎn huí jiā, shì ma? 女孩晚上10点回家，是吗？

8 You are singing well, aren't you? Nǐ chàng dé hěn hǎo, bùshì ma? 你唱得很好，不是吗？

9 He is seeing you, isn't he? Tā zài kàn nǐ, bùshì ma? 他在看你，不是吗？

10 We are eating bread, aren't we? Wǒmen zhèngzài chī miànbāo, bùshì ma? 我们正在吃面包，不是吗？

Type 3E. I have done, haven't I? Wǒ yǐjīng wánchéngle, bùshì ma? 我已经完成了，不是吗？

1 The Sun has risen, hasn't it? Tàiyáng yǐjīng shēng qǐ, bùshì ma? 太阳已经升起，不是吗？

2 Mother has cooked, hasn't she? Māmā zuò fànle, bùshì ma? 妈妈做饭了，不是吗？

3 Thief has stolen at night, hasn't he? Xiǎotōu zài wǎnshàng tōule dōngxī, bùshì ma? 小偷在晚上偷了东西，不是**吗**？

4 Father has gone to office, hasn't he? Fùqīn qù bàngōngshìle, shì ma? 父亲去办公室了，是**吗**？

5 Mr Rabi has taught students, hasn't he? Lā bǐ xiānshēng jiàoguò xuéshēng, bùshì ma? 拉比先生教过学生，不是**吗**？

6 I have taken light food in the morning, haven't I? Wǒ zǎoshang chīle qīngdàn de shíwù, bùshì ma? 我早上吃了清淡的食物，不是**吗**？

7 The girl has come home at 10 PM at night, hasn't she? Nàgè nǚhái wǎnshàng 10 diǎn cái huí jiā, bùshì ma? 那个女孩晚上10点才回家，不是**吗**？

8 You have sung well, haven't you? Nǐ chàng dé hěn hǎo, bùshì ma? 你唱得很好，不是**吗**？

9 He has seen you, hasn't he? Tā jiànguò nǐ, bùshì ma? 他见过你，不是**吗**？

10 We have eaten bread, haven't we? Wǒmen chīguò miànbāo, bùshì ma? 我**们**吃过面包，不是**吗**？

Type 4E. I did, didn't I? Wǒ zuò dàole, bùshì ma? 我做到了，不是**吗**？

1 The Sun rose, didn't it? Tàiyáng shēng qǐláile, bùshì ma? 太阳升起来了，不是**吗**？

2 Mother cooked, didn't she? Māmā zuò fàn, bùshì ma? **妈妈**做**饭**，不是**吗**？

3 Thief stole at night, didn't he? Xiǎotōu wǎnshàng tōu de, bùshì ma? 小偷晚上偷的，不是**吗**？

4 Father went to office, didn't he? Fùqīn qù bàngōngshìle, shì ma? 父亲去办公室了，是**吗**？

5 Mr Rabi taught students, didn't he? Lā bǐ xiānshēng jiàoguò xuéshēng, bùshì ma? 拉比先生教过学生，不是**吗**？

6 I took light food in the morning, didn't I? Wǒ zǎoshang chī qīngdàn de shíwù, bùshì ma? 我早上吃清淡的食物，不是**吗**？

7 The girl came home at 10 PM at night, didn't she? Nàgè nǚhái wǎnshàng 10 diǎn cái huí jiā, shì ma? 那个女孩晚上10点才回家，是**吗**？

8 You sang well, didn't you? Nǐ chàng dé hěn hǎo, bùshì ma? 你唱得很好，不是**吗**？

9 He saw you, didn't he? Tā kànjiàn nǐle, bùshì ma? 他看见你了，不是**吗**？

10 We ate bread, didn't we? Wǒmen chīle miànbāo, bùshì ma? 我们吃了面包，不是吗？

Type 5E. I was doing, wan't I? Wǒ zài zuò, bùshì ma? 我在做，不是吗？

1 The Sun was rising, wan't it? Tàiyáng zhèngzài shēng qǐ, bùshì ma? 太阳正在升起，不是吗？

2 Mother was cooking, wan't she? Māmā zhèngzài zuò fàn, shì ma? 妈妈正在做饭，是吗？

3 Thief was stealing at night, wan't he? Xiǎotōu zài wǎnshàng tōu dōngxī, shì ma? 小偷在晚上偷东西，是吗？

4 Father was going to office, wan't he? Fùqīn yào qù bàngōngshì, shì ma? 父亲要去办公室，是吗？

5 Mr Rabi was teaching students, wan't he? Lā bǐ xiānshēng zhèngzài jiào xuéshēng, shì ma? 拉比先生正在教学生，是吗？

6 I was taking light food in the morning, wan't I? Wǒ zǎoshang chī qīngdàn de shíwù, duì ma? 我早上吃清淡的食物，对吗？

7 The girl was coming home at 10 PM at night, wan't she? Nàgè nǚhái wǎnshàng 10 diǎn cái huí jiā, shì ma? 那个女孩晚上 10 点才回家，是吗？

8 You were singing well, ware't you? Nǐ chàng dé hěn hǎo, shì ma? 你唱得很好，是吗？

9 He was seeing you, wan't he? Tā zài jiàn nǐ, shì ma? 他在见你，是吗？

10 We were eating bread, weren't we? Wǒmen zhèngzài chī miànbāo, bùshì ma? 我们正在吃面包，不是吗？

Type 6E. I will do, won't I? Wǒ huì zuò de, bùshì ma? 我会做的，不是吗？

1 The Sun will rise, won't it? Tàiyáng huì shēng qǐ, bùshì ma? 太阳会升起，不是吗？

2 Mother will cook, won't she? Māmā huì zuò fàn, bùshì ma? 妈妈会做饭，不是吗？

3 Thief will steal at night, won't he? Xiǎotōu huì zài wǎnshàng tōu dōngxī, bùshì ma? 小偷会在晚上偷东西，不是吗？

4 Father will go to office, won't he? Fùqīn huì qù bàngōngshì, shì ma? 父亲会去办公室，是吗？

5 Mr Rabi will teach students, won't he? Lā bǐ xiānshēng huì jiào xuéshēng, bùshì ma? 拉比先生会教学生，不是吗？

6 I will take light food in the morning, won't I? Wǒ zǎoshang huì chī qīngdàn de shíwù, duì ma? 我早上会吃清淡的食物，对**吗**？

7 The girl will come home at 10 PM at night, won't she? Nǚhái wǎnshàng 10 diǎn huì huí jiā, bùshì ma? 女孩晚上10点会回家，不是**吗**？

8 You will sing well, won't you? Nǐ huì chàng dé hěn hǎo, bùshì ma? 你会唱得很好，不是**吗**？

9 He will see you, won't he? Tā huìjiàn nǐ de, bùshì ma? 他会见你的，不是**吗**？

10 We will eat bread, won't we? Wǒmen huì chī miànbāo, bùshì ma? 我**们**会吃面包，不是**吗**？

Type 7E. I will be doing, won't we? Wǒ huì zuò de, bùshì ma? 我会做的，不是**吗**？

1 The Sun will be rising, won't he? Tàiyáng huì shēng qǐ, bùshì ma? 太阳会升起，不是**吗**？

2 Mother will be cooking, won't she? Māmā huì zuò fàn, shì ma? **妈妈**会做**饭**，是**吗**？

3 Thief will be stealing at night, won't he? Xiǎotōu huì zài wǎnshàng tōu dōngxī, bùshì ma? 小偷会在晚上偷东西，不是**吗**？

4 Father will be going to office, won't he? Fùqīn yào shàngrènle, shì ma? 父亲要上任了，是**吗**？

5 Mr Rabi will be teaching students, won't he? Lā bǐ xiānshēng huì jiào xuéshēng, duì ma? 拉比先生会教学生，对**吗**？

6 I will be taking light food in the morning, won't I? Wǒ zǎoshang huì chī qīngdàn de shíwù, bùshì ma? 我早上会吃清淡的食物，不是**吗**？

7 The girl will be coming home at 10 PM at night, won't she? Nàgè nǚhái wǎnshàng 10 diǎn huì huí jiā, shì ma? 那个女孩晚上 10 点会回家，是**吗**？

8 You will be singing well, won't you? Nǐ huì chàng dé hěn hǎo, bùshì ma? 你会唱得很好，不是**吗**？

9 He will be seeing you, won't he? Tā huì lái kàn nǐ de, bùshì ma? 他会来看你的，不是**吗**？

10 We will be eating bread, won't we? Wǒmen yào chī miànbāo, bùshì ma? 我**们**要吃面包，不是**吗**？

Type 8E. I will have done, won't I? Wǒ huì zuò dào de, bùshì ma? 我会做到的，不是**吗**？

1 The Sun will have risen, won't it? Tàiyáng huì shēng qǐ, bùshì ma? 太阳会升起，不是吗？

2 Mother will have cooked, won't she? Māmā huì zuò fàn de, shì ma? 妈妈会做饭的，是吗？

3 Thief will have stolen at night, won't he? Xiǎotōu wǎnshàng huì tōu dōngxī de, bùshì ma? 小偷晚上会偷东西的，不是吗？

4 Father will have gone to office, won't he? Fùqīn huì qù bàngōngshì de, bùshì ma? 父亲会去办公室的，不是吗？

5 Mr Rabi will have taught students, won't he? Lā bǐ xiānshēng huì jiào xuéshēng de, bùshì ma? 拉比先生会教学生的，不是吗？

6 I will have taken light food in the morning, won't I? Wǒ zǎoshang huì chī qīngdàn de shíwù, bùshì ma? 我早上会吃清淡的食物，不是吗？

7 The girl will have come home at 10 PM at night, won't she? Nàgè nǚhái wǎnshàng 10 diǎn huì huí jiā, bùshì ma? 那个女孩晚上 10 点会回家，不是吗？

8 You will have sung well, won't you? Nǐ huì chàng dé hěn hǎo, bùshì ma? 你会唱得很好，不是吗？

9 He will have seen you, won't he? Tā huì kàn dào nǐ de, bùshì ma? 他会看到你的，不是吗？

10 We will have eaten bread, won't I? Wǒmen huì chī miànbāo de, bùshì ma? 我们会吃面包的，不是吗？

Type 9E. I can do, can't I? Wǒ kěyǐ, bùshì ma? 我可以，不是吗？

1 The Sun can rise, can't it? Tàiyáng kěyǐ shēng qǐ, bùshì ma? 太阳可以升起，不是吗？

2 Mother can cook, can't she? Māmā huì zuò fàn, bùshì ma? 妈妈会做饭，不是吗？

3 Thief can steal at night, can't he? Xiǎotōu kěyǐ zài wǎnshàng tōu dōngxī, bùshì ma? 小偷可以在晚上偷东西，不是吗？

4 Father can go to office, can't he? Fùqīn kěyǐ qù bàngōngshì, bùshì ma? 父亲可以去办公室，不是吗？

5 Mr Rabi can teach students, can't he? Lā bǐ xiānshēng kěyǐ jiào xuéshēng, bùshì ma? 拉比先生可以教学生，不是吗？

6 I can take light food in the morning, can't I? Wǒ zǎoshang kěyǐ chī qīngdàn de shíwù, bùshì ma? 我早上可以吃清淡的食物，不是吗？

7 The girl can come home at 10 PM at night, can't she? Nàgè nǚhái wǎnshàng 10 diǎn kěyǐ huí jiā, bùshì ma? 那个女孩晚上10点可以回家，不是吗？

8 You can sing well, can't you? Nǐ chàng dé hěn hǎo, bùshì ma? 你唱得很好，不是吗？

9 He can see you, can't he? Tā néng kàn dào nǐ, bùshì ma? 他能看到你，不是吗？

10 We can eat bread, can't I? Wǒmen kěyǐ chī miànbāo, bùshì ma? 我们可以吃面包，不是吗？

Type 10E. I could do, couldn't I? Wǒ kěyǐ, bùshì ma? 我可以，不是吗？

1 The Sun could rise, couldn't it? Tàiyáng kěyǐ shēng qǐ, bùshì ma? 太阳可以升起，不是吗？

2 Mother could cook, couldn't she? Māmā huì zuò fàn, bùshì ma? 妈妈会做饭，不是吗？

3 Thief could steal at night, couldn't he? Xiǎotōu kěyǐ zài wǎnshàng tōu dōngxī, bùshì ma? 小偷可以在晚上偷东西，不是吗？

4 Father could go to office, couldn't he? Fùqīn kěyǐ qù bàngōngshì, bùshì ma? 父亲可以去办公室，不是吗？

5 Mr Rabi could teach students, couldn't he? Lā bǐ xiānshēng kěyǐ jiào xuéshēng, bùshì ma? 拉比先生可以教学生，不是吗？

6 I could take light food in the morning, couldn't I? Wǒ zǎoshang kěyǐ chī qīngdàn de shíwù, bùshì ma? 我早上可以吃清淡的食物，不是吗？

7 The girl could come home at 10 PM at night, couldn't she? Nàgè nǚhái wǎnshàng 10 diǎn kěyǐ huí jiā, bùshì ma? 那个女孩晚上 10 点可以回家，不是吗？

8 You could sing well, couldn't you? Nǐ chàng dé hěn hǎo, bùshì ma? 你唱得很好，不是吗？

9 He could see you, couldn't he? Tā néng kànjiàn nǐ, bùshì ma? 他能看见你，不是吗？

10 We could eat bread, couldn't I? Wǒmen kěyǐ chī miànbāo, bùshì ma? 我们可以吃面包，不是吗？

Type 1F. I don't do, do I? Wǒ bù zuò, shì ma? 我不做，是吗？

1 The Sun doesn't rise, does it? Tàiyáng bù huì shēng qǐ, shì ma? 太阳不会升起，是吗？

2 Mother doesn't cook, does she? Māmā bù zuò fàn, shì ma? 妈妈不做饭，是吗？

3 Thief doesn't steal at night, does he? Xiǎotōu wǎnshàng bù huì tōu dōngxī ba? 小偷晚上不会偷东西吧？

4 Father doesn't go to office, does he? Fùqīn bù qù bàngōngshì, shì ma? 父亲不去办公室，是吗？

5 Mr Rabi doesn't teach students, does he? Lā bǐ xiānshēng bù jiào xuéshēng, shì ma? 拉比先生不教学生，是吗？

6 I don't take light food in the morning, do I? Wǒ zǎoshang bù chī qīngdàn de shíwù, shì ma? 我早上不吃清淡的食物，是吗？

7 The girl doesn't come home at 10 PM at night, does she? Nàgè nǚhái wǎnshàng 10 diǎn bù huí jiā, shì ma? 那个女孩晚上10点不回家，是吗？

8 You don't sing well, do you? Nǐ chàng dé bù hǎo, shì ma? 你唱得不好，是吗？

9 He doesn't see you, does he? Tā kàn bùjiàn nǐ, shì ma? 他看不见你，是吗？

10 We don't eat bread, do I? Wǒmen bù chī miànbāo, shì ma? 我们不吃面包，是吗？

Type 2F. I am not doing, am I? Wǒ bùshì zài zuò, shì ma? 我不是在做，是吗？

1 The Sun is not rising, is it? Tàiyáng méiyǒu shēng qǐ, shì ma? 太阳没有升起，是吗？

2 Mother is not cooking, is she? Māmā bù huì zuò fàn, shì ma? 妈妈不会做饭，是吗？

3 Thief is not stealing at night, is he? Xiǎotōu bù huì zài wǎnshàng tōu dōngxī ba? 小偷不会在晚上偷东西吧？

4 Father is not going to office, is he? Fùqīn bù huì qù bàngōngshì, shì ma? 父亲不会去办公室，是吗？

5 Mr Rabi is not teaching students, is he? Rabi xiānshēng bùshì zài jiào xuéshēng, shì ma? Rabi 先生不是在教学生，是吗？

6 I am not taking light food in the morning, am I? Wǒ zǎoshang méiyǒu chī qīngdàn de shíwù, shì ma? 我早上没有吃清淡的食物，是吗？

7 The girl is not coming home at 10 PM at night, is she? Nǚhái wǎnshàng 10 diǎn bù huì huí jiā, shì ma? 女孩晚上10点不会回家，是吗？

8 You are not singing well, are you? Nǐ chànggē bù hǎotīng ba? 你唱歌不好听吧？

9 He is not seeing you, is he? Tā méiyǒu jiàn nǐ, shì ma? 他没有见你，是吗？

10 We are not eating bread, are we? Wǒmen bùshì zài chī miànbāo, shì ma? 我们不是在吃面包，是吗？

Type 3F. I have not done, have I? Wǒ méiyǒu zuò, shì ma? 我没有做，是吗？

1 The Sun has not risen, has it? Tàiyáng hái méi shēng qǐ, shì ma? 太阳还没升起，是吗？

2 Mother has not cooked, has she? Māmā méiyǒu zuò fàn, shì ma? 妈妈没有做饭，是吗？

3 Thief has not stolen at night, has he? Xiǎotōu wǎnshàng méiyǒu tōu dōngxī ba? 小偷晚上没有偷东西吧？

4 Father has not gone to office, has he? Fùqīn méiyǒu qù bàngōngshì, shì ma? 父亲没有去办公室，是吗？

5 Mr Rabi has not taught students, has he? Lā bǐ xiānshēng méiyǒu jiàoguò xuéshēng, shì ma? 拉比先生没有教过学生，是吗？

6 I have not taken light food in the morning, have I? Wǒ zǎoshang méiyǒu chī qīngdàn de shíwù, shì ma? 我早上没有吃清淡的食物，是吗？

7 The girl has not come home at 10 PM at night, has she? Nàgè nǚhái wǎnshàng 10 diǎn hái méi huí jiā, shì ma? 那个女孩晚上10点还没回家，是吗？

8 You have not sung well, have you? Nǐ chàng dé bù hǎo, shì ma? 你唱得不好，是吗？

9 He has not seen you, has he? Tā méiyǒu jiànguò nǐ, shì ma? 他没有见过你，是吗？

10 We have not eaten bread, have we? Wǒmen méi chīguò miànbāo ba? 我们没吃过面包吧？

Type 4F. I did not do, did I? Wǒ méiyǒu zuò, shì ma? 我没有做，是吗？

1 The Sun didn't rise, did it? Tàiyáng méiyǒu shēng qǐ, shì ma? 太阳没有升起，是吗？

2 Mother didn't cook, did she? Māmā bù huì zuò fàn, shì ma? 妈妈不会做饭，是吗？

3 Thief didn't steal at night, did he? Xiǎotōu wǎnshàng bù huì tōu dōngxī ba? 小偷晚上不会偷东西吧？

4 Father didn't go to office, did he? Fùqīn méiyǒu qù bàngōngshì, shì ma? 父亲没有去办公室，是吗？

5 Mr Rabi didn't teach students, did he? Lā bǐ xiānshēng méiyǒu jiào xuéshēng, shì ma? 拉比先生没有教学生，是吗？

6 I didn't take light food in the morning, did I? Wǒ zǎoshang méiyǒu chī qīngdàn de shíwù, shì ma? 我早上没有吃清淡的食物，是吗？

7 The girl didn't come home 10 PM at night, did she? Nàgè nǚhái wǎnshàng 10 diǎn méiyǒu huí jiā, shì ma? 那个女孩晚上10点没有回家，是吗？

8 You didn't sing well, did you? Nǐ chàng dé bù hǎo, shì ma? 你唱得不好，是吗？

9 He didn't see you, did he? Tā méi kànjiàn nǐ, shì ma? 他没看见你，是吗？

10 We didn't eat bread, did we? Wǒmen méiyǒu chī miànbāo, shì ma? 我们没有吃面包，是吗？

Type 5F. I was not doing, was I? Wǒ méiyǒu zuò, shì ma? 我没有做，是吗？

1 The Sun was not rising, was it? Tàiyáng méiyǒu shēng qǐ, shì ma? 太阳没有升起，是吗？

2 Mother was not cooking, was she? Māmā méiyǒu zuò fàn, shì ma? 妈妈没有做饭，是吗？

3 Thief was not stealing at night, was he? Xiǎotōu bù huì zài wǎnshàng tōu dōngxī ba? 小偷不会在晚上偷东西吧？

4 Father was not going to office, was he? Fùqīn bù huì qù bàngōngshì, shì ma? 父亲不会去办公室，是吗？

5 Mr Rabi was not teaching students, was he? Lā bǐ xiānshēng bùshì zài jiào xuéshēng, shì ma? 拉比先生不是在教学生，是吗？

6 I was not taking light food in the morning, was I? Wǒ zǎoshang méiyǒu chī qīngdàn de shíwù, shì ma? 我早上没有吃清淡的食物，是吗？

7 The girl was not coming home at 10 PM at night, was she? Nàgè nǚhái wǎnshàng 10 diǎn bù huì huí jiā, shì ma? 那个女孩晚上10点不会回家，是吗？

8 You were not singing well, were you? Nǐ chàng dé bù hǎo, shì ma? 你唱得不好，是吗？

9 He was not seeing you, was he? Tā méiyǒu jiàn nǐ, shì ma? 他没有见你，是吗？

10 We were not eating bread, were we? Wǒmen méiyǒu chī miànbāo, shì ma? 我们没有吃面包，是吗？

Type 6F. I will not do, will I? Wǒ bù huì zuò de, shì ma? 我不会做的，是吗？

1 The Sun will not rise, will it? Tàiyáng bù huì shēng qǐ, shì ma? 太阳不会升起，是吗？

2 Mother will not cook, will she? Māmā bù huì zuò fàn, shì ma? 妈妈不会做饭，是吗？

3 Thief will not steal at night, will he? Xiǎotōu bù huì zài wǎnshàng tōu dōngxī ba? 小偷不会在晚上偷东西吧？

4 Father will not go to office, will he? Fùqīn bù huì qù bàngōngshì, shì ma? 父亲不会去办公室，是吗？

5 Mr Rabi will not teach students, will he? Lā bǐ xiānshēng bù huì jiào xuéshēng ba? 拉比先生不会教学生吧？

6 I will not take light food in the morning, will I? Wǒ zǎoshang bù huì chī qīngdàn de shíwù, shì ma? 我早上不会吃清淡的食物，是吗？

7 The girl will not come home at 10 PM at night, will she? Nàgè nǚhái wǎnshàng 10 diǎn bù huì huí jiā ba? 那个女孩晚上10点不会回家吧？

8 You will not sing well, will you? Nǐ bù huì chànggē hǎotīng ba? 你不会唱歌好听吧？

9 He will not see you, will he? Tā bù huìjiàn nǐ ba? 他不会见你吧？

10 We will not eat bread, will we? Wǒmen bù huì chī miànbāo, shì ma? 我们不会吃面包，是吗？

Type 7F. I will be doing, will I? Wǒ huì zuò de, shì ma? 我会做的，是吗？

1 The Sun will be rising, will it? Tàiyáng huì shēng qǐ, shì ma? 太阳会升起，是吗？

2 Mother will be cooking, will she? Māmā huì zuò fàn, shì ma? 妈妈会做饭，是吗？

3 Thief will be stealing at night, will he? Xiǎotōu huì zài wǎnshàng tōu dōngxī, shì ma? 小偷会在晚上偷东西，是吗？

4 Father will be going to office, will he? Fùqīn yào qù bàngōngshì, shì ma? 父亲要去办公室，是吗？

5 Mr Rabi will be teaching students, will he? Lā bǐ xiānshēng huì jiào xuéshēng, shì ma? 拉比先生会教学生，是吗？

6 I will be taking light food in the morning, will I? Wǒ zǎoshang huì chī qīngdàn de shíwù, duì ma? 我早上会吃清淡的食物，对吗？

7 The girl will not be coming home at 10 PM at night, will she? Nàgè nǚhái wǎnshàng 10 diǎn bù huì huí jiā, shì ma? 那个女孩晚上10点不会回家，是吗？

8 You will not be singing well, will you? Nǐ bù huì chànggē hěn hǎotīng ba? 你不会唱歌很好听吧？

9 He will not be seeing you, will he? Tā bù huìjiàn nǐ de ba? 他不会见你的吧？

10 We will not be eating bread, will we? Wǒmen bù huì chī miànbāo ba? 我们不会吃面包吧？

Type 8F. I will not have done, will I? Wǒ bù huì zuò de, shì ma? 我不会做的，是吗？

1 The Sun will not have risen, will it? Tàiyáng bù huì shēng qǐ ba? 太阳不会升起吧？

2 Mother will not have cooked, will she? Māmā bù huì zuò fàn ba? 妈妈不会做饭吧？

3 Thief will not have stolen at night, will he? Xiǎotōu bù huì zài wǎnshàng tōu dōngxī ba? 小偷不会在晚上偷东西吧？

4 Father will not have gone to office, will he? Fùqīn bù huì qù bàngōngshì ba? 父亲不会去办公室吧？

5 Mr Rabi will not have taught students, will he? Lā bǐ xiānshēng bù huì jiào xuéshēng ba? 拉比先生不会教学生吧？

6 I will not have taken light food in the morning, will I? Wǒ zǎoshang bù huì chī qīngdàn de shíwù, duì ma? 我早上不会吃清淡的食物，对吗？

7 The girl will not have come home at 10 PM at night, will she? Nàgè nǚhái bù huì zài wǎnshàng 10 diǎn huí jiā ba? 那个女孩不会在晚上 10 点回家吧？

8 You will not have sung well, will you? Nǐ bù huì chàng dé hěn hǎo ba? 你不会唱得很好吧？

9 He will not have seen you, will he? Tā bù huìjiànguò nǐ ba? 他不会见过你吧？

10 We will not have eaten bread, will we? Wǒmen bù huì chī miànbāo ba? 我们不会吃面包吧？

Type 9F. I can not do, can I? Wǒ zuò bù dào, kěyǐ ma? 我做不到，可以吗？

1 The Sun can not rise, can he? Tàiyáng bù huì shēng qǐ, shì ma? 太阳不会升起，是吗？

2 Mother can not cook, can she? Māmā bù huì zuò fàn, shì ma? 妈妈不会做饭，是吗？

3 Thief can not steal at night, can he? Xiǎotōu wǎnshàng bùnéng tōu, duì ma? 小偷晚上不能偷，对吗？

4 Father can not go to office, can he? Fùqīn bùnéng qù bàngōngshì, shì ma? 父亲不能去办公室，是吗？

5 Mr Rabi can not teach students, can he? Lā bǐ xiānshēng bùnéng jiào xuéshēng, shì ma? 拉比先生不能教学生，是吗？

6 I can not take light food in the morning, can I? Wǒ zǎoshang bùnéng chī qīngdàn de shíwù, kěyǐ ma? 我早上不能吃清淡的食物，可以吗？

7 The girl can not come home at 10 PM at night, can she? Nǚhái wǎnshàng 10 diǎn bùnéng huí jiā, shì ma? 女孩晚上10点不能回家，是吗？

8 You can not sing well, can you? Nǐ bù huì chànggē hǎotīng ba? 你不会唱歌好听吧？

9 He can not see you, can he? Tā kàn bù dào nǐ, shì ma? 他看不到你，是吗？

10 We can not eat bread, can we? Wǒmen bùnéng chī miànbāo, shì ma? 我们不能吃面包，是吗？

Type 10F. I could not do, could I? Wǒ zuò bù dào, shì ma? 我做不到，是吗？

1 The Sun could not rise, could it? Tàiyáng bù huì shēng qǐ, shì ma? 太阳不会升起，是吗？

2 Mother could not cook, could she? Māmā bù huì zuò fàn, shì ma? 妈妈不会做饭，是吗？

3 Thief could not steal at night, could he? Xiǎotōu wǎnshàng bù huì tōu dōngxī ba? 小偷晚上不会偷东西吧？

4 Father could not go to office, could he? Fùqīn bùnéng qù bàngōngshì, shì ma? 父亲不能去办公室，是吗？

5 Mr Rabi could not teach students, could he? Lā bǐ xiānshēng bùnéng jiào xuéshēng, shì ma? 拉比先生不能教学生，是吗？

6 I could not take light food in the morning, could I? Wǒ zǎoshang bùnéng chī qīngdàn de shíwù, shì ma? 我早上不能吃清淡的食物，是吗？

7 The girl could not come home at 10 PM at night, could she? Nàgè nǚhái wǎnshàng 10 diǎn bùnéng huí jiā, shì ma? 那个女孩晚上10点不能回家，是吗？

8 You could not sing well, could you? Nǐ chàng dé bù hǎo, shì ma? 你唱得不好，是吗？

9 He could not see you, could he? Tā kàn bùjiàn nǐ, shì ma? 他看不见你，是吗？

10 We could not eat bread, could we? Wǒmen bùnéng chī miànbāo, shì ma? 我们不能吃面包，是吗？

Type 1G. What do I do? Wǒ gāi zěnme bàn? 我该怎么办？

1 When does the Sun rise? Tàiyáng shénme shíhòu shēng qǐ? 太阳什么时候升起？

2 Whom does mother cook for? Māmā wèi shéi zuò fàn? 妈妈为谁做饭？

3 How does thief steal at night? Xiǎotōu wǎnshàng zěnme tōu dōngxī? 小偷晚上怎么偷东西？

4 Where does Father go? Bàba qù nǎ'erle? 爸爸去哪儿了？

5 What does Mr Rabi teach students for? Lā bǐ xiānshēng jiào xuéshēng shénme? 拉比先生教学生什么？

6 Whom do I take light food in the morning with? Wǒ zǎoshang hé shéi yīqǐ chī qīngdàn de shíwù? 我早上和谁一起吃清淡的食物？

7 When does the girl come home? Nǚhái shénme shíhòu huí jiā? 女孩什么时候回家？

8 How do you sing? Nǐ zěnme chànggē? 你怎么唱歌？

9 Who sees you? Shéi jiàn nǐ? 谁见你？

10 Who eat bread? Shéi chī miànbāo? 谁吃面包？

Type 2G. What am I doing ? Wǒ zài zuò shénme? 我在做什么 ？

1 When is the Sun rising ? Tàiyáng shénme shíhòu shēng qǐ? 太阳什么时候升起？

2 Whom is mother cooking for? Māmā wèi shéi zuò fàn? 妈妈为谁做饭？

3 When is the thief stealing? Xiǎotōu shénme shíhòu tōu dōngxī? 小偷什么时候偷东西？

4 Where is father going? Bàba qù nǎ'er? 爸爸去哪儿？

5 Whom is Mr Rabi teaching? Lā bǐ xiānshēng zài jiào shéi? 拉比先生在教谁？

6 What am I taking in the morning? Wǒ zǎoshang chī shénme? 我早上吃什么？

7 Where is the girl going 10 PM at night? Wǎnshàng 10 diǎn nǚhái qù nǎ'er? 晚上10点女孩去哪儿？

8 Where are you singing? Nǐ zài nǎlǐ chànggē? 你在哪里唱歌？

9 Why is he seeing you? Tā wèishéme yào jiàn nǐ? 他为什么要见你？

10 Whom are we are eating bread with? Wǒmen hé shéi yīqǐ chī miànbāo? 我们和谁一起吃面包？

Type 3G. What have I done ? Wǒ zuòle shénme? 我做了什么 ？

1 When has the Sun risen ? Tàiyáng shénme shíhòu shēng qǐ? 太阳什么时候升起？

2 What has mother cooked ? Māmā zhǔle shénme? 妈妈煮了什么？

3 Where has the thief stolen at night ? Xiǎotōu wǎnshàng qù nǎ'er tōu de? 小偷晚上去哪儿偷的？

4 Why has father gone to office ? Fùqīn wèishéme qù bàngōngshì? 父亲为什么去办公室？

5 Whom has Mr Rabi taught? Lā bǐ xiānshēng jiàoguò shéi? 拉比先生教过谁？

6 What have I taken in the morning ? Wǒ zǎoshang chīle shénme? 我早上吃了什么？

7 Whom has the girl returned home with 10 PM at night ? Wǎnshàng 10 diǎn, nǚhái shì shéi huí jiā de? 晚上10点，女孩是谁回家的？

8 How have you sung well? Nǐ zěnme chàng dé hǎo? 你怎么唱得好？

9 Who have seen you ? Shéi jiànguò nǐ? 谁见过你？

10 What have we eaten? Wǒmen chīle shénme? 我们吃了什么？

Type 4G. What did I do? Wǒ zuòle shénme? 我做了什么？

1 When did the Sun rise? Tàiyáng shénme shíhòu shēng qǐ de? 太阳什么时候升起的？

2 Whom did mother cook for? Māmā wèi shéi zuò fàn? 妈妈为谁做饭？

3 When did the thief steal? Xiǎotōu shénme shíhòu tōu de? 小偷什么时候偷的？

4 How did father go to office? Fùqīn shì zěnme qù bàngōngshì de? 父亲是怎么去办公室的？

5 What did Mr Rabi teach? Lā bǐ xiānshēng jiàole shénme? 拉比先生教了什么？

6 When did I take light food? Wǒ shénme shíhòu chī qīngdàn de shíwùle? 我什么时候吃清淡的食物了？

7 When did the girl come home? Nǚhái shénme shíhòu huí jiā de? 女孩什么时候回家的？

8 Where did you sing? Nǐ zài nǎlǐ chàng de? 你在哪里唱的？

9 Why did he see you for? Tā wèishéme yào jiàn nǐ? 他为什么要见你？

10 Who ate bread? Shéi chīle miànbāo? 谁吃了面包？

Type 5G. What was I doing? Wǒ zài zuò shénme? 我在做什么？

1 Where was the Sun rising? Tàiyáng cóng nǎlǐ shēng qǐ? 太阳从哪里升起？

2 Where was mother cooking? Māmā zài nǎlǐ zuò fàn? 妈妈在哪里做饭？

3 What was the thief stealing? Xiǎotōu tōule shénme dōngxī? 小偷偷了什么东西？

4 Whom was father going to office with? Fùqīn yào hé shéi yīqǐ shàngbān? 父亲要和谁一起上班？

5 What was Mr Rabi teaching? Lā bǐ xiānshēng jiàole shénme? 拉比先生教了什么？

6 What was I taking light food in the morning for? Wǒ zǎoshang chī qīngdàn de shíwù shì wèile shénme? 我早上吃清淡的食物是为了什么？

7 Who was coming home 10 PM at night? Wǎnshàng 10 diǎn shéi huí jiā? 晚上10点谁回家？

8 Whom were you singing for? Nǐ wèi shéi chànggē? 你为谁唱歌？

9 Why was he looking at you? Tā wèishéme kànzhe nǐ? 他为什么看着你？

10 Why were we eating bread for? Wǒmen wèishéme yào chī miànbāo? 我们为什么要吃面包？

Type 6G. What will I do? Wǒ gāi zěnme bàn? 我该怎么办？

1 When will the Sun rise? Tàiyáng shénme shíhòu shēng qǐ? 太阳什么时候升起？

2 Why will mother cook for? Wèishéme māmā huì zuò fàn? 为什么妈妈会做饭？

3 Why will the thief steal at night? Wèishéme xiǎotōu huì zài wǎnshàng tōu dōngxī? 为什么小偷会在晚上偷东西？

4 How will father go to office? Bàba zěnme qù bàngōngshì? 爸爸怎么去办公室？

5 Whom will Mr Rabi teach? Lā bǐ xiānshēng huì jiào shéi? 拉比先生会教谁？

6 Who will take light food in the morning? Shéi huì zài zǎoshang chī qīngdàn de shíwù? 谁会在早上吃清淡的食物？

7 Whom will the girl return home 10 PM at night? Wǎnshàng 10 diǎn nǚhái huì huí jiā zhǎo shéi? 晚上10点女孩会回家找谁？

8 When will you sing? Nǐ shénme shíhòu chànggē? 你什么时候唱歌？

9 Why will he see you? Tā wèishéme yào jiàn nǐ? 他为什么要见你？

10 How many roti will we eat? Wǒmen yào chī duōshǎo kǎoròu? 我们要吃多少烤肉？

Type 7G. What will I be doing? Wǒ huì zuò shénme? 我会做什么？

1 How will the Sun be rising? Tàiyáng jiàng rúhé shēng qǐ? 太阳将如何升起？

2 Why will mother be cooking? Wèishéme māmā huì zuò fàn? 为什么妈妈会做饭？

3 What will thief be stealing at night? Xiǎotōu wǎnshàng huì tōu shénme? 小偷晚上会偷什么？

4 Why will father be going to office? Bàba wèishéme yào qù bàngōngshì? 爸爸为什么要去办公室？

5 Whom will Mr Rabi be teaching? Lā bǐ xiānshēng jiāng jiào shéi? 拉比先生将教谁？

6 Why will I be taking light food in the morning? Wèishéme wǒ zǎoshang yào chī qīngdàn de shíwù? 为什么我早上要吃清淡的食物？

7 Whom will the girl be returning home 10 PM at night? Wǎnshàng 10 diǎn, nǚhái huì hé shéi huí jiā? 晚上10点，女孩会和谁回家？

8 How will you be singing well? Nǐ zěnme chàng dé hǎo? 你怎么唱得好？

9 Why will he be seeing you? Tā wèishéme yào jiàn nǐ? 他为什么要见你？

10 How long will we be eating bread? Wǒmen hái yào chī miànbāo duōjiǔ? 我们还要吃面包多久？

Type 8G. What will I have done? Wǒ huì zěnme zuò? 我会怎么做？

1 When will the Sun have risen? Tàiyáng shénme shíhòu shēng qǐ? 太阳什么时候升起？

2 Whom will mother have cooked for? Māmā huì wèi shéi zuò fàn? 妈妈会为谁做饭？

3 When will the thief have stolen? Xiǎotōu shénme shíhòu tōule? 小偷什么时候偷了？

4 Whom will father have gone to office with? Fùqīn huì hé shéi yīqǐ qù bàngōngshì? 父亲会和谁一起去办公室？

5 What will Mr Rabi have taught? Lā bǐ xiānshēng huì jiào shénme? 拉比先生会教什么？

6 What will I have taken in the morning? Wǒ zǎoshang huì chī shénme? 我早上会吃什么？

7 When will the girl have returned home? Nǚhái shénme shíhòu huí jiā? 女孩什么时候回家？

8 Who will have sung? Shéi huì chànggē? 谁会唱歌？

9 Who will have seen you? Shéi huì kàn dào nǐ? 谁会看到你？

10 How long will we have eaten roti? Wǒmen hái néng chī duōjiǔ de roti? 我们还能吃多久的roti？

Type 9G. What can I do? Wǒ néng zuò shénme? 我能做什么？

1 When can the Sun rise? Tàiyáng shénme shíhòu kěyǐ shēng qǐ? 太阳什么时候可以升起？

2 Whom can mother cook for? Māmā kěyǐ wéi shéi zuò fàn? 妈妈可以为谁做饭？

3 Where can the thief steal at night? Xiǎotōu wǎnshàng qù nǎlǐ tōu? 小偷晚上去哪里偷？

4 When can father go to office? Bàba shénme shíhòu kěyǐ shàngbān? 爸爸什么时候可以上班？

5 What can Mr Rabi teach? Lā bǐ xiānshēng néng jiào shénme? 拉比先生能教什么？

6 What can I take in the morning? Wǒ zǎoshang kěyǐ chī shénme? 我早上可以吃什么？

7 When can the girl return home? Nǚhái shénme shíhòu kěyǐ huí jiā? 女孩什么时候可以回家？

8 When can you sing? Shénme shíhòu kěyǐ chànggē? 什么时候可以唱歌？

9 Who can see you? Shéi néng kàn dào nǐ? 谁能看到你？

10 What can we eat? Wǒmen kěyǐ chī shénme? 我们可以吃什么？

Type 10G. What could I do? Wǒ néng zuò shénme? 我能做什么？

1 When could the Sun rise? Tàiyáng shénme shíhòu shēng qǐ? 太阳什么时候升起？

2 What could mother cook? Māmā huì zhǔ shénme? 妈妈会煮什么？

3 Where could the thief steal at night? Xiǎotōu wǎnshàng huì qù nǎlǐ tōu? 小偷晚上会去哪里偷？

4 Whom could father go to office with? Fùqīn kěyǐ hé shéi yīqǐ qù bàngōngshì? 父亲可以和谁一起去办公室？

5 Which subject could Mr Rabi teach? Lā bǐ xiānshēng kěyǐ jiào shénme kēmù? 拉比先生可以教什么科目？

6 What could I take in the morning? Wǒ zǎoshang kěyǐ chī shénme? 我早上可以吃什么？

7 When could the girl return home? Nǚhái shénme shíhòu kěyǐ huí jiā? 女孩什么时候可以回家？

8 Which song could you sing? Nǐ huì chàng nǎ shǒu gē? 你会唱哪首歌？

9 When could he see you? Tā shénme shíhòu néng jiàn dào nǐ? 他什么时候能见到你？

10 What could we eat? Wǒmen néng chī shénme? 我们能吃什么？

WH Negative Question

Type 1H. What do I not do? Wǒ bù zuò shénme? 我不做什么？

1 When does the Sun not rise? Tàiyáng shénme shíhòu bù shēng qǐ? 太阳什么时候不升起？

2 Whom does mother not cook for? Māmā bù gěi shéi zuò fàn? 妈妈不给谁做饭？

3 How does thief not steal at night? Xiǎotōu wǎnshàng zěnme bù tōu? 小偷晚上怎么不偷？

4 Where does father not go? Fùqīn bù qù nǎlǐ? 父亲不去哪里？

5 What does Mr Rabi not teach students for? Lā bǐ xiānshēng bù jiào xuéshēng shénme? 拉比先生不教学生什么？

6 Whom do I not take light food in the morning with? Wǒ zǎoshang bù hé shéi chī qīngdàn de shíwù? 我早上不和谁吃清淡的食物？

7 When does the girl not come home? Nǚhái shénme shíhòu bù huí jiā? 女孩什么时候不回家？

8 How do you not sing? Bù chànggē zěnme bàn? 不唱歌怎么办？

9 Who does not see you? Shéi bùjiàn nǐ? 谁不见你？

10 Who do not eat bread? Shéi bù chī miànbāo? 谁不吃面包？

Type 2H. What am I not doing ? Wǒ bù zuò shénme? 我不做什么？

1 When is the Sun not rising? Tàiyáng shénme shíhòu bù shēng qǐ? 太阳什么时候不升起？

2 Whom is mother not cooking for? Māmā bù wéi shéi zuò fàn? 妈妈不为谁做饭？

3 When is the thief not stealing? Zéi shénme shíhòu bù tōu? 贼什么时候不偷？

4 Where is father not going? Bàba bù qù nǎlǐ? 爸爸不去哪里？

5 Whom is Mr Rabi not teaching? Lā bǐ xiānshēng bù jiào shéi? 拉比先生不教谁？

6 What am I not taking in the morning? Wǒ zǎoshang bù chī shénme? 我早上不吃什么？

7 Where is the girl not going 10 PM at night? Wǎnshàng 10 diǎn gūniáng bù qù nǎlǐ? 晚上10点姑娘不去哪里？

8 Where are you not singing? Nǐ zài nǎlǐ bù chànggē? 你在哪里不唱歌？

9 Why is he not seeing you? Tā wèishéme bùjiàn nǐ? 他为什么不见你？

10 Whom are we not eating bread with? Wǒmen bù hé shéi yīqǐ chī miànbāo? 我们不和谁一起吃面包？

Type 3H. What have I not done ? Wǒ hái méiyǒu zuò shénme? 我还没有做什么？

1 When has the Sun not risen ? Tàiyáng shénme shíhòu méiyǒu shēng qǐ? 太阳什么时候没有升起？

2 What has mother not cooked ? Māmā yǒu shé me méi zhǔguò? 妈妈有什么没煮过？

3 Where has the thief not stolen at night? Xiǎotōu yèlǐ méi tōu dào nǎlǐ qù? 小偷夜里没偷到哪里去？

4 Why has father not gone to office ? Fùqīn wèishéme bù qù bàngōngshì? 父亲为什么不去办公室？

5 Whom has Mr Rabi not taught? Lā bǐ xiānshēng méiyǒu jiàoguò shéi? 拉比先生没有教过**谁**？

6 What have I not taken in the morning ? Wǒ zǎoshang méiyǒu chī shénme? 我早上没有吃什么？

7 Whom has the girl not returned home with 10 PM at night ? Wǎnshàng 10 diǎn, nǚhái hái méiyǒu huí dào shéi jiā? 晚上10点，女孩还没有回到**谁**家？

8 How have you not sung well? Nǐ zěnme chàng dé bù hǎo? 你怎么唱得不好？

9 Who have not seen you ? Shéi méi jiànguò nǐ? **谁**没见过你？

10 What have we not eaten? Wǒmen méiyǒu chīguò shèn me? 我**们**没有吃过什么？

Type 4H. What did I not do? Wǒ méiyǒu zuò shénme? 我没有做什么？

1 When did the Sun not rise? Tàiyáng shénme shíhòu méiyǒu shēng qǐ? 太阳什么时候没有升起？

2 Whom did mother not cook for? Māmā méiyǒu wéi shéi zuò fàn? **妈妈**没有**为谁**做**饭**？

3 When did the thief not steal? Xiǎotōu shénme shíhòu bù tōu dōngxīle? 小偷什么时候不偷东西了？

4 How did father not go to office? Bàba zěnme méi qù bàngōngshì? 爸爸怎么没去办公室？

5 What did Mr Rabi not teach? Lā bǐ xiānshēng méiyǒu jiào shénme? 拉比先生没有教什么？

6 When did I not take light food? Wǒ shénme shíhòu bù chī qīngdàn de shíwùle? 我什么时候不吃清淡的食物了？

7 When did the girl not come home? Nǚhái shénme shíhòu bù huí jiā de? 女孩什么时候不回家的？

8 Where did you not sing? Nǎlǐ méi chàng? 哪里没唱？

9 Why did he not see you for? Tā zěnme méi jiàn nǐ? 他怎么没见你？

10 Who did not eat bread? Shéi méi chīguò miànbāo? **谁**没吃过面包？

Type 5H. What was I not doing? Wǒ méiyǒu zuò shénme? 我没有做什么？

1 Where was the Sun not rising? Tàiyáng méiyǒu shēng qǐ dì dìfāng shì nǎlǐ? 太阳没有升起的地方是哪里？

2 Where was mother not cooking? Māmā nǎlǐ bù zuò fàn? 妈妈哪里不做饭？

3 What was the thief not stealing? Xiǎotōu méiyǒu tōu shénme? 小偷没有偷什么？

4 Whom was father not going to office with? Fùqīn bù qù hé shéi yīqǐ shàngbān? 父亲不去和谁一起上班？

5 What was Mr Rabi not teaching? Lā bǐ xiānshēng méiyǒu jiào shénme? 拉比先生没有教什么？

6 What was I not taking light food in the morning for? Wǒ zǎoshang bù chī qīngdàn de shíwù shì wèile shénme? 我早上不吃清淡的食物是为了什么？

7 Who was not coming home 10 PM at night? Shéi wǎnshàng 10 diǎn bù huí jiā? 谁晚上10点不回家？

8 Whom were you not singing for? Nǐ bùshì wèi shéi chànggē de? 你不是为谁唱歌的？

9 Why was he not looking at you? Tā wèishéme bù kàn nǐ? 他为什么不看你？

10 Why were we not eating bread for? Wèishéme wǒmen bù chī miànbāo? 为什么我们不吃面包？

Type 6H. What will I not do? Wǒ bù huì zuò shénme? 我不会做什么？

1 When will the Sun not rise? Tàiyáng shénme shíhòu bù shēng qǐ? 太阳什么时候不升起？

2 Why will mother not cook for? Wèishéme māmā bù huì zuò fàn? 为什么妈妈不会做饭？

3 Why will the thief not steal at night? Wèishéme xiǎotōu wǎnshàng bù huì tōu dōngxī? 为什么小偷晚上不会偷东西？

4 How will father not go to office? Bàba bù qù bàngōngshì zěnme bàn? 爸爸不去办公室怎么办？

5 Whom will Mr Rabi not teach? Lā bǐ xiānshēng bù huì jiào shéi? 拉比先生不会教谁？

6 Who will not take light food in the morning? Shéi zǎoshang bù chī qīngdàn de shíwù? 谁早上不吃清淡的食物？

7 Whom will the girl not return home 10 PM at night? Wǎnshàng 10 diǎn nǚhái bù huí jiā shéi jiā? 晚上10点女孩不回家谁家？

8 When will you not sing? Nǐ shénme shíhòu bù chànggē? 你什么时候不唱歌？

9 Why will he not see you? Tā wèishéme bùjiàn nǐ? 他为什么不见你？

10 How many roti will we not eat? Wǒmen bù chī duōshǎo kǎoròu? 我们不吃多少烤肉？

Type 7H. What will I not be doing? Wǒ bù huì zuò shénme? 我不会做什么？

1 How will the Sun not be rising? Tàiyáng zěnme huì bù shēng qǐ? 太阳怎么会不升起？

2 Why will mother not be cooking? Wèishéme māmā bù zuò fàn? 为什么妈妈不做饭？

3 What will thief not be stealing at night? Xiǎotōu wǎnshàng bù huì tōu shénme? 小偷晚上不会偷什么？

4 Why will father not be going to office? Wèishéme fùqīn bù qù bàngōngshì? 为什么父亲不去办公室？

5 Whom will Mr Rabi not be teaching? Lā bǐ xiānshēng bù huì jiào shéi? 拉比先生不会教谁？

6 Why will I not be taking light food in the morning? Wèishéme wǒ zǎoshang bù chī qīngdàn de shíwù? 为什么我早上不吃清淡的食物？

7 Whom will the girl not be returning home 10 PM at night? Wǎnshàng 10 diǎn nǚhái bù huí jiā de shì shéi? 晚上10点女孩不回家的是谁？

8 How will you not be singing well? Nǐ zěnme huì chàng bù hǎo? 你怎么会唱不好？

9 Why will he not be seeing you? Tā wèishéme bù lái kàn nǐ? 他为什么不来看你？

10 How long will we not be eating bread? Wǒmen yào duōjiǔ bù chī miànbāo? 我们要多久不吃面包？

Type 8H. What will I not have done? Shénme shì wǒ méiyǒu zuò de? 什么是我没有做的？

1 When will the Sun not have risen? Tàiyáng shénme shíhòu bù huì shēng qǐ? 太阳什么时候不会升起？

2 Whom will mother not have cooked for? Māmā bù gěi shéi zuò fàn? 妈妈不给谁做饭？

3 When will the thief not have stolen? Xiǎotōu shénme shíhòu bù tōule? 小偷什么时候不偷了？

4 Whom will father not have gone to office with? Fùqīn bù huì hé shéi yīqǐ qù bàngōngshì? 父亲不会和谁一起去办公室？

5 What will Mr Rabi not have taught? Lā bǐ xiānshēng bù huì jiào shénme? 拉比先生不会教什么？

6 What will I not have taken in the morning? Wǒ zǎoshang bù huì chī shénme? 我早上不会吃什么？

7 When will the girl not have returned home? Nǚhái shénme shíhòu bù huí jiā? 女孩什么时候不回家？

8 Who will not have sung? Shéi bù huì chànggē? 谁不会唱歌？

9 Who will not have seen you? Shéi méi jiànguò nǐ? 谁没见过你？

10 How long will we not have eaten roti? Wǒmen duōjiǔ méiyǒu chīguò roti? 我们多久没有吃过roti？

Type 9H. What can I not do? Wǒ bùnéng zuò shénme? 我不能做什么？

1 When can the Sun not rise? Tàiyáng shénme shíhòu bù shēng qǐ? 太阳什么时候不升起？

2 Whom can mother not cook for? Māmā bùnéng wéi shéi zuò fàn? 妈妈不能为谁做饭？

3 Where can the thief not steal at night? Xiǎotōu yèlǐ nǎlǐ bù tōu? 小偷夜里哪里不偷？

4 When can father not go to office? Bàba shénme shíhòu kěyǐ bù qù bàngōngshì? 爸爸什么时候可以不去办公室？

5 What can Mr Rabi not teach? Lā bǐ xiānshēng bùnéng jiào shénme? 拉比先生不能教什么？

6 What can I not take in the morning? Wǒ zǎoshang bùnéng chī shénme? 我早上不能吃什么？

7 When can the girl not return home? Nǚhái shénme shíhòu bùnéng huí jiā? 女孩什么时候不能回家？

8 When can you not sing? Shénme shíhòu bùnéng chànggē? 什么时候不能唱歌？

9 Who can not see you? Shéi kàn bù dào nǐ? 谁看不到你？

10 What can we not eat? Wǒmen bùnéng chī shénme? 我们不能吃什么？

Type 10H. What could I not do? Wǒ bùnéng zuò shénme? 我不能做什么？

1 When could the Sun not rise? Tàiyáng shénme shíhòu bù shēng qǐ? 太阳什么时候不升起？

2 What could mother not cook? Māmā yǒu shé me bùnéng zuò de? 妈妈有什么不能做的？

3 Where could the thief not steal at night? Xiǎotōu yèlǐ nǎlǐ bù tōu? 小偷夜里哪里不偷？

4 Whom could father not go to office with? Fùqīn bùnéng hé shéi yīqǐ qù bàngōngshì? 父亲不能和谁一起去办公室？

5 Which subject could Mr Rabi not teach? Lā bǐ xiānshēng bùnéng jiào nǎ mén kè? 拉比先生不能教哪门课？

6 What could I not take in the morning? Wǒ zǎoshang bùnéng chī shénme? 我早上不能吃什么？

7 When could the girl not return home? Nǚhái shénme shíhòu bùnéng huí jiā? 女孩什么时候不能回家？

8 Which song could you not sing? Nǐ bùnéng chàng nǎ shǒu gē? 你不能唱哪首歌？

9 When could he not see you? Tā shénme shíhòu bùnéng jiàn nǐ? 他什么时候不能见你？

10 What could we not eat? Wǒmen bùnéng chī shénme? 我们不能吃什么？

Chapter 5

1 I do. Wǒ zuò. 我做。

2 I am doing. Wǒ zài zuò. 我在做。

3 I have done. Wǒ yǐjīng zuò hǎole. 我已经做好了。

4 I did. Wǒ zuò dàole. 我做到了。

5 I was doing. Wǒ zài zuò. 我在做。

6 I will do. Wǒ huì zuò. 我会做。

7 I will be doing. Wǒ huì zuò de. 我会做的。

8 I will have done. Wǒ huì zuò dào de. 我会做到的。

9 I can do. Wǒ kěyǐ. 我可以。

10 I could do. Wǒ kěyǐ zuò. 我可以做。

11 I could have done. Wǒ běnlái kěyǐ zuò dào de. 我本来可以做到的。

12 I may do. Wǒ kěyǐ. 我可以。

13 I may be doing. Wǒ kěnéng zhèngzài zuò. 我可能正在做。

14 I may have done. Wǒ kěnéng yǐjīng zuò dàole. 我可能已经做到了。

15 I might do. Wǒ kěnéng huì. 我可能会。

16 I might be doing Wǒ kěnéng zhèngzài zuò 我可能正在做

17 I must do. wǒ bìxū zhèyàng zuò. 我必须这样做。

18 I must be doing. Wǒ yīdìng shì zài zuò. 我一定是在做。

19 I must have done. Wǒ yīdìng zuò dàole. 我一定做到了。

20 I should do. Wǒ yīnggāi zuò. 我**应该**做。

21 I should be doing. Wǒ yīnggāi zuò de. 我**应该**做的。

22 I should have done. Wǒ yīnggāi zuò de. 我**应该**做的。

23 I should have been doing. Wǒ yīnggāi yīzhí zài zuò. 我**应该**一直在做。

24 I used to do. Wǒ céngjīng zuòguò. 我曾经做过。

25 I am used to doing. / I am in the habit of doing. Wǒ xíguànle. / Wǒ yǒu zhèyàng zuò de xíguàn. 我**习惯**了。/我有这样做的**习惯**。

26 I was used to doing. / I was in the habit of doing. Wǒ yǐjīng xíguànle. / Wǒ yǒu zhèyàng zuò de xíguàn. 我已经**习惯**了。/我有这样做的**习惯**。

27 I am supposed to do. Wǒ yīnggāi zuò de. 我**应该**做的。

28 I was supposed to do. Wǒ yīnggāi zuò de. 我**应该**做的。

29 I have to do. Wǒ yào zuò. 我要做。

30 I had to do. Wǒ bìxū zuò. 我必**须**做。

31 I have had to do. Wǒ bùdé bù zhèyàng zuò. 我不得不这样做。

32 I got to do. Wǒ dé zuò. 我得做。

33 I got to be doing. Wǒ dé zuò. 我得做。

34 I want you to do. Wǒ yào nǐ zuò. 我要你做。

35 I wanted you to do. Wǒ xiǎng ràng nǐ zuò. 我想**让**你做。

36 You seem to do. Nǐ sìhū kěyǐ. 你似乎可以。

37 You seem to have done. Nǐ hǎoxiàng zuò dàole. 你好像做到了。

38 You seemed to do. Nǐ sìhū zuò dàole. 你似乎做到了。

39 You seemed to have done. Nǐ hǎoxiàng zuò dàole. 你好像做到了。

40 I am able to do. Wǒ yǒu nénglì zuò dào. 我有能力做到。

41 I was able to do. Wǒ nénggòu zuò dào. 我能够做到。

42 I am about to do. Wǒ zhèng yào zuò. 我正要做。

43 I was about to do. Wǒ zhèng yào qù zuò. 我正要去做。

44 I do do. Wǒ quèshí. 我确实。

45 Let me do. Ràng wǒ zuò. **让**我做。

46 Let me have to do. Ràng wǒ bùdé bù zuò. **让**我不得不做。

47 I try to do. Wǒ shìzhe qù zuò. 我**试**着去做。

48 I tried to do. Wǒ shìzhe zuò. 我**试**着做。

49 I love to do. Wǒ xǐhuān zuò. 我喜欢做。

50 I loved to do. Wǒ xǐhuān zuò. 我喜欢做。

51 I like to be doing. Wǒ xǐhuān zuò. 我喜欢做。
52 I liked to be doing. Wǒ xǐhuān zuò. 我喜欢做。
53 I want to be doing. Wǒ xiǎng zuò. 我想做。
54 I wanted to be doing. Wǒ xiǎng zuò. 我想做。
55 I like to do. Wǒ xǐhuān zuò. 我喜欢做。
56 I liked to do. Wǒ xǐhuān zuò. 我喜欢做。
57 I want to do. Wǒ xiǎng yào zuò. 我想要做。
58 I wanted to do. Wǒ xiǎng zuò. 我想做。
59 I need to do. Wǒ xūyào qù zuò. 我需要去做。
60 I needed to do. Wǒ xūyào zuò. 我需要做。
61 I need to be doing. Wǒ xūyào zuò. 我需要做。
62 I needed to be doing. Wǒ xūyào zuò. 我需要做。
63 I hope to do. Wǒ xīwàng zuò dào. 我希望做到。
64 I hoped to do. Wǒ xīwàng zhèyàng zuò. 我希望这样做。
65 I dare to do. Wǒ gǎn zuò. 我敢做。
66 I dared to do. Wǒ gǎn zuò. 我敢做。
1 I don't do. Wǒ bù zuò. 我不做。
2 I am not doing. Wǒ bùshì zài zuò. 我不是在做。
3 I have not done. Wǒ méiyǒu zuòguò. 我没有做过。
4 I didn't do. Wǒ méiyǒu zuò. 我没有做。
5 I was not doing. Wǒ bùshì zài zuò. 我不是在做。
6 I will not do. Wǒ bù huì. 我不会。
7 I will not be doing. Wǒ bù huì zuò de. 我不会做的。
8 I will not have done. Wǒ bù huì zuò de. 我不会做的。
9 I can not do. Wǒ bùnéng zuò. 我不能做。
10 I could not do. Wǒ zuò bù dào. 我做不到。
11 I could not have done. Wǒ zuò bù dào. 我做不到。
12 I may not do. Wǒ kěnéng bù huì. 我可能不会。
13 I may not be doing. Wǒ kěnéng bù huì zuò. 我可能不会做。
14 I may not have done. Wǒ kěnéng méiyǒu zuòguò. 我可能没有做过。
15 I might not do. Wǒ kěnéng bù huì. 我可能不会。
16 I might not be doing Wǒ kěnéng bù huì zuò 我可能不会做
17 I must not do. wǒ yīdìng bùnéng zhèyàng zuò. 我一定不能这样做。
18 I must not be doing. Wǒ yīdìng bùshì zài zuò. 我一定不是在做。
19 I must not have done. Wǒ yīdìng méiyǒu zuòguò. 我一定没有做过。
20 I should not do. Wǒ bù yìng gāi zhèyàng zuò. 我不**应该**这样做。

21 I should not be doing. Wǒ bù yìng gāi zhèyàng zuò. 我不**应该**这样做。

22 I should not have done. Wǒ bù yìng gāi zhèyàng zuò. 我不**应该**这样做。

23 I should not have been doing. Wǒ bù yìng gāi zhèyàng zuò. 我不**应该**这样做。

24 I didn't use to do. Wǒ méiyǒu zuò. 我没有做。

25 I am not used to doing. / I am in the habit of doing. Wǒ bù xíguàn zhèyàng zuò. / Wǒ yǒu zhèyàng zuò de xíguàn. 我不**习惯**这样做。 / 我有这样做的**习惯**。

26 I was not used to doing. / I was in the habit of doing. Wǒ bù xíguàn zhèyàng zuò. / Wǒ yǒu zhèyàng zuò de xíguàn. 我不**习惯**这样做。 / 我有这样做的**习惯**。

27 I am not supposed to do. Wǒ bù yìng gāi zhèyàng zuò. 我不**应该**这样做。

28 I was not supposed to do. Wǒ bù yìng gāi zhèyàng zuò. 我不**应该**这样做。

29 I don't have to do. Wǒ bùbì zhèyàng zuò. 我不必这样做。

30 I didn't have to do. Wǒ bùbì zhèyàng zuò. 我不必这样做。

31 I don't have had to do. Wǒ bùbì zhèyàng zuò. 我不必这样做。

32 I didn't get to do. Wǒ méi dé zuò. 我没得做。

33 I didn't get to be doing. Wǒ méiyǒu qù zuò. 我没有去做。

34 I don't want you to do. Wǒ bù xīwàng nǐ zhèyàng zuò. 我不希望你这样做。

35 I didn't want you to do. Wǒ bùxiǎng ràng nǐ zhèyàng zuò. 我不想**让**你这样做。

36 You don't seem to do. Nǐ sìhū méiyǒu. 你似乎没有。

37 You don't seem to have done. Nǐ sìhū méiyǒu zuò dào. 你似乎没有做到。

38 You didn't seem to do. Nǐ hǎoxiàng méiyǒu. 你好像没有。

39 You didn't seem to have done. Nǐ sìhū méiyǒu zuò dào. 你似乎没有做到。

40 I am not able to do. Wǒ zuò bù dào. 我做不到。

41 I was not able to do. Wǒ méi néng zuò dào. 我没能做到。

42 I am not about to do. Wǒ bù dǎsuàn zuò. 我不打算做。

43 I was not about to do. Wǒ bù dǎsuàn zuò. 我不打算做。

44 I do never do. Wǒ cóng bù zhèyàng zuò. 我从不这样做。

45 Don't let me do. Bùyào ràng wǒ zuò. 不要让我做。

46 Don't let me have to do. Bùyào ràng wǒ bùdé bù zuò. 不要让我不得不做。

47 I don't try to do. / I try not to do. Wǒ bù chángshì qù zuò. / Wǒ jǐnliàng bù zuò. 我不尝试去做。 / 我尽量不做。

48 I didn't try to do. / I tried not to do. Wǒ méiyǒu chángshì qù zuò. / Wǒ shìzhe bù zhèyàng zuò. 我没有尝试去做。 / 我试着不这样做。

49 I don't love to do. Wǒ bù xǐhuān zuò. 我不喜欢做。

50 I didn't love to do. Wǒ bù xǐhuān zuò. 我不喜欢做。

51 I don't like to be doing. Wǒ bù xǐhuān zuò. 我不喜欢做。

52 I didn't like to be doing. Wǒ bù xǐhuān zuò. 我不喜欢做。

53 I don't want to be doing. Wǒ bùxiǎng zuò. 我不想做。

54 I didn't want to be doing. Wǒ bùxiǎng zuò. 我不想做。

55 I don't like to do. Wǒ bù xǐhuān zuò. 我不喜欢做。

56 I didn't like to do. Wǒ bù xǐhuān zuò. 我不喜欢做。

57 I don't want to do. Wǒ bùxiǎng zuò. 我不想做。

58 I didn't want to do. Wǒ bùxiǎng zuò. 我不想做。

59 I don't need to do. Wǒ bù xūyào zuò. 我不需要做。

60 I didn't need to do. Wǒ bù xūyào zuò. 我不需要做。

61 I don't need to be doing. Wǒ bù xūyào zuò. 我不需要做。

62 I didn't need to be doing. Wǒ bù xūyào zuò. 我不需要做。

63 I don't hope to do. Wǒ bù xīwàng zhèyàng zuò. 我不希望这样做。

64 I didn't hope to do. Wǒ bù xīwàng zhèyàng zuò. 我不希望这样做。

65 I don't dare to do. Wǒ bù gǎn zuò. 我不敢做。

66 I didn't dare to do. Wǒ bù gǎn zuò. 我不敢做。

1 Do I do? Wǒ zuò ma? 我做吗？

2 AM I doing? Wǒ zài zuò shénme? 我在做什么？

3 Have I done? Wǒ zuò dàole ma? 我做到了吗？

4 Did I do? Wǒ zuòle ma? 我做了吗？

5 Was I doing? Wǒ zài zuò shénme? 我在做什么？

6 Will I do? Wǒ huì zuò ma? 我会做吗？

7 Will I be doing? Wǒ huì zuò ma? 我会做吗？

8 Will I have done? Wǒ huì zuò ma? 我会做吗？

9 Can I do? Wǒ kěbù kěyǐ zuò? 我可不可以做？

10 Could I do? Wǒ kěyǐ ma? 我可以吗？

11 Could I have done? Wǒ néng zuò dào ma? 我能做到吗？

12 May I do? Wǒ kěyǐ ma? 我可以吗？

13 May I be doing? Wǒ kěyǐ zài zuò shénme ma? 我可以在做什么吗？

14 May I have done? Wǒ kěyǐ zuò ma? 我可以做吗？

15 Might I do? Wǒ kěyǐ ma? 我可以吗？

16 Might I be doing? Wǒ kěnéng zài zuò shénme? 我可能在做什么？

17 Must I do? Wǒ bìxū zhèyàng zuò ma? 我必须这样做吗？

18 Must I be doing? Wǒ bìxū zuò ma? 我必须做吗？

19 Must I have done? Wǒ bìxū zuò ma? 我必须做吗？

20 Should I do? Wǒ yīnggāi zuò ma? 我应该做吗？

21 Should I be doing? Wǒ yīnggāi zuò shénme? 我应该做什么？

22 Should I have done? Wǒ yīnggāi zuò ma? 我应该做吗？

23 Should I have been doing? Wǒ yīnggāi yīzhí zài zuò shénme? 我应该一直在做什么？

24 Did I use to do? Wǒ yǐqián zuòguò ma? 我以前做过吗？

25 AM I used to doing? / Am I in the habit of doing? Wǒ xíguànle ma? / Wǒ yǒu zhèyàng zuò de xíguàn ma? 我习惯了吗？ / 我有这样做的习惯吗？

26 Was I used to doing? / Was I in the habit of doing? Wǒ xíguànle ma? / Wǒ yǒu zhèyàng zuò de xíguàn ma? 我习惯了吗？ / 我有这样做的习惯吗？

27 AM I supposed to do? Wǒ yīnggāi zěnme zuò? 我应该怎么做？

28 Was I supposed to do? Wǒ yīnggāi zěnme zuò? 我应该怎么做？

29 Do I have to do? Wǒ bìxū zhèyàng zuò ma? 我必须这样做吗？

30 Did I have to do? Wǒ bìxū zhèyàng zuò ma? 我必须这样做吗？

31 Do I have had to do? Wǒ bùdé bù zhèyàng zuò ma? 我不得不这样做吗？

32 Did I get to do? Wǒ yǒu zuò ma? 我有做吗？

33 Did I get to be doing? Wǒ yǒu zuòshì ma? 我有做事吗？

34 Do I want you to do? Wǒ yào nǐ zuò shénme? 我要你做什么？

35 Did I want you to do? Wǒ xiǎng ràng nǐ zuò ma? 我想让你做吗？

36 Do you seem to do? Nǐ hǎoxiàng ne? 你好像呢？

37 Do you seem to have done? Nǐ hǎoxiàng zuò dàole? 你好像做到了？

38 Did you seem to do? Nǐ hǎoxiàng zuò dàole? 你好像做到了？

39 Did you seem to have done? Nǐ hǎoxiàng zuò dàole? 你好像做到了？

40 AM I able to do? Wǒ néng zuò dào ma? 我能做到吗？

41 Was I able to do? Wǒ néng zuò dào ma? 我能做到吗？
42 AM I about to do? Wǒ yào zuò ma? 我要做吗？
43 Was I about to do? Wǒ yào zuò ma? 我要做吗？
44 Do I do do? Wǒ zuò ma? 我做吗？
45
46
47 Do I try to do? Wǒ chángshì zuò ma? 我尝试做吗？
48 Did I try to do? Wǒ shìguò ma? 我试过吗？
49 Do I love to do? Wǒ xǐhuān zuò ma? 我喜欢做吗？
50 Did I love to do? Wǒ xǐhuān zuò ma? 我喜欢做吗？
51 Do I like to be doing? Wǒ xǐhuān zuòshì ma? 我喜欢做事吗？
52 Did I like to be doing? Wǒ xǐhuān zuò ma? 我喜欢做吗？
53 Do I want to be doing? Wǒ xiǎng zuò ma? 我想做吗？
54 Did I want to be doing? Wǒ xiǎng zuò ma? 我想做吗？
55 Do I like to do? Wǒ xǐhuān zuò shénme? 我喜欢做什么？
56 Did I like to do? Wǒ xǐhuān zuò ma? 我喜欢做吗？
57 Do I want to do? Wǒ xiǎng zuò ma? 我想做吗？
58 Did I want to do? Wǒ xiǎng zuò ma? 我想做吗？
59 Do I need to do? Wǒ xūyào zuò ma? 我需要做吗？
60 Did I need to do? Wǒ xūyào zuò ma? 我需要做吗？
61 Do I need to be doing? Wǒ xūyào zuò ma? 我需要做吗？
62 Did I need to be doing? Wǒ xūyào zuò ma? 我需要做吗？
63 Do I hope to do? Wǒ xīwàng zhèyàng zuò ma? 我希望这样做吗？
64 Did I hope to do? Wǒ xīwàng zhèyàng zuò ma? 我希望这样做吗？
65 Do I dare to do? Wǒ gǎn zuò ma? 我敢做吗？
66 Did I dare to do? Wǒ gǎn zuò ma? 我敢做吗？
1 Do I not do? Wǒ bù zuò ma? 我不做吗？
2 AM I not doing? Wǒ bùshì zài zuò ma? 我不是在做吗？
3 Have I not done? Wǒ méiyǒu zuò ma? 我没有做吗？
4 Did I not do? Wǒ méiyǒu zuò ma? 我没有做吗？
5 Was I not doing? Wǒ bùshì zài zuò ma? 我不是在做吗？
6 Will I not do? Wǒ bù huì ma? 我不会吗？
7 Will I not be doing? Wǒ bù huì zuò ma? 我不会做吗？
8 Will I not have done? Wǒ bù huì zuò ma? 我不会做吗？
9 Can I not do? Wǒ kěyǐ bù zuò ma? 我可以不做吗？

10 Could I not do? Wǒ kěyǐ bù zuò ma? 我可以不做吗？

11 Could I not have done? Wǒ kěyǐ bù zuò ma? 我可以不做吗？

12 May I not do? Wǒ kěyǐ bù zuò ma? 我可以不做吗？

13 May I not be doing? Wǒ kěyǐ bù zuò ma? 我可以不做吗？

14 May I not have done? Wǒ kěnéng méiyǒu zuòguò ma? 我可能没有做过吗？

15 Might I not do? Wǒ kěyǐ bù zuò ma? 我可以不做吗？

16 Might I not be doing? Wǒ kěyǐ bù zuò ma? 我可以不做吗？

17 Must I not do? Wǒ bìxū bù zhèyàng zuò ma? 我必须不这样做吗？

18 Must I not be doing? Wǒ bìxū bù zuò ma? 我必须不做吗？

19 Must I not have done? Wǒ yīdìng méiyǒu zuòguò ma? 我一定没有做过吗？

20 Should I not do? Wǒ bù yìng gāi zuò ma? 我不应该做吗？

21 Should I not be doing? Wǒ bù yìng gāi zuò ma? 我不应该做吗？

22 Should I not have done? Wǒ bù yìng gāi zuò ma? 我不应该做吗？

23 Should I not have been doing? Wǒ bù yìng gāi yīzhí zài zuò ma? 我不应该一直在做吗？

24 Did I not use to do? Wǒ méi yòngguò ma? 我没用过吗？

25 AM I not used to doing? / Am I not in the habit of doing? Wǒ bù xíguàn ma? / Wǒ méiyǒu zhèyàng zuò de xíguàn ma? 我不习惯吗？ / 我没有这样做的习惯吗？

26 Was I not used to doing? / Was I not in the habit of doing? Shì wǒ bù xíguàn ma? / Nándào wǒ méiyǒu zhèyàng zuò de xíguàn? 是我不习惯吗？ / 难道我没有这样做的习惯？

27 AM I not supposed to do? Wǒ bù yìng gāi zhèyàng zuò ma? 我不应该这样做吗？

28 Was I not supposed to do? Wǒ bùshì yīnggāi zuò de ma? 我不是应该做的吗？

29 Do I not have to do? Nándào wǒ bùyòng ma? 难道我不用吗？

30 Did I not have to do? Wǒ bùshì bìxū zuò ma? 我不是必须做吗？

31 Do I not have had to do? Nándào wǒ méiyǒu bànfǎ ma? 难道我没有办法吗？

32 Did I not get to do? Wǒ méiyǒu zuò ma? 我没有做吗？

33 Did I not get to be doing? Wǒ méiyǒu zuò ma? 我没有做吗？

34 Do I not want you to do? Wǒ bùxiǎng nǐ zuò shénme? 我不想你做什么？

35 Did I not want you to do? Wǒ bùshì yào nǐ zuò ma? 我不是要你做吗？

36 Do you not seem to do? Hǎoxiàng bù zuò ma? 好像不做吗？

37 Do you not seem to have done? Hǎoxiàng méiyǒu zuò ma? 好像没有做吗？

38 Did you not seem to do? Nǐ hǎoxiàng méi zuò? 你好像没做？

39 Did you not seem to have done? Nǐ hǎoxiàng méi zuòguò? 你好像没做过？

40 AM I not able to do? Wǒ zuò bù dào ma? 我做不到吗？

41 Was I not able to do? Wǒ zuò bù dào ma? 我做不到吗？

42 AM I not about to do? Wǒ bù zhǔnbèi zuò ma? 我不准备做吗？

43 Was I not about to do? Wǒ bùshì yào zuò shénme ma? 我不是要做什么吗？

44 Do I do never do? Wǒ cónglái bu zuò ma? 我从来不做吗？

45

46

47 Do I not try to do? Nándào wǒ bù shì shì ma? 难道我不试试吗？

48 Did I not try to do? Wǒ méiyǒu chángshì zuò ma? 我没有尝试做吗？

49 Do I not love to do? Nándào wǒ bù ài zuò ma? 难道我不爱做吗？

50 Did I not love to do? Wǒ bù ài zuò ma? 我不爱做吗？

51 Do I not like to be doing? Wǒ bù xǐhuān bèi zuò ma? 我不喜欢被做吗？

52 Did I not like to be doing? Wǒ bù xǐhuān zuò ma? 我不喜欢做吗？

53 Do I not want to be doing? Wǒ bùxiǎng zuò ma? 我不想做吗？

54 Did I not want to be doing? Wǒ bùxiǎng zuò ma? 我不想做吗？

55 Do I not like to do? Wǒ bù xǐhuān zuò shénme? 我不喜欢做什么？

56 Did I not like to do? Wǒ bù xǐhuān zuò ma? 我不喜欢做吗？

57 Do I not want to do? Wǒ bùxiǎng zuò ma? 我不想做吗？

58 Did I not want to do? Wǒ bùxiǎng zuò ma? 我不想做吗？

59 Do I not need to do? Wǒ bù xūyào zuò ma? 我不需要做吗？

60 Did I not need to do? Wǒ bù xūyào zuò ma? 我不需要做吗？

61 Do I not need to be doing? Wǒ bù xūyào zuò ma? 我不需要做吗？

62 Did I not need to be doing? Wǒ bù xūyào zuò ma? 我不需要做吗？

63 Do I not hope to do? Nándào wǒ bù xīwàng ma? 难道我不希望吗？

64 Did I not hope to do? Nándào wǒ méiyǒu xīwàng ma? 难道我没有希望吗？

65 Do I not dare to do? Nándào wǒ bù gǎn ma? 难道我不敢吗？

66 Did I not dare to do? Wǒ bù gǎn zuò ma? 我不敢做吗？

Chapter 6

1 I do. Wǒ zuò. 我做。

The beggar begs. Qǐgài qǐtǎo. 乞丐乞讨。

2 I am doing. Wǒ zài zuò. 我在做。

The beggar is begging. Qǐgài zài qǐtǎo. 乞丐在乞讨。

3 I have done. Wǒ yǐjīng zuò hǎole. 我已经做好了。

The beggar has begged. Qǐgài qǐtǎole. 乞丐乞讨了。

4 I did. Wǒ zuò dàole. 我做到了。

The beggar begged. Qǐgài kěnqiú dào. 乞丐恳求道。

5 I was doing. Wǒ zài zuò. 我在做。

The beggar was begging. Qǐgài zài qǐtǎo. 乞丐在乞讨。

6 I will do. Wǒ huì zuò. 我会做。

The beggar will beg. Qǐgài huì qǐtǎo. 乞丐会乞讨。

7 I will be doing. Wǒ huì zuò de. 我会做的。

The beggar will be begging. Qǐgài huì qǐtǎo. 乞丐会乞讨。

8 I will have done. Wǒ huì zuò dào de. 我会做到的。

The beggar will have begged. Qǐgài huì qǐtǎo de. 乞丐会乞讨的。

9 I can do. Wǒ kěyǐ. 我可以。

The beggar can beg. Qǐgài kěyǐ qǐtǎo. 乞丐可以乞讨。

10 I could do. Wǒ kěyǐ zuò. 我可以做。

The beggar could beg. Qǐgài kěyǐ qǐtǎo. 乞丐可以乞讨。

11 I could have done. Wǒ běnlái kěyǐ zuò dào de. 我本来可以做到的。

The beggar could have begged. Qǐgài běnlái kěyǐ qǐtǎo de. 乞丐本来可以乞讨的。

12 I may do. Wǒ kěyǐ. 我可以。

The beggar may beg. Qǐgài kěnéng huì qǐtǎo. 乞丐可能会乞讨。

13 I may be doing. Wǒ kěnéng zhèngzài zuò. 我可能正在做。

The beggar may be begging. Qǐgài kěnéng zài qǐtǎo. 乞丐可能在乞讨。

14 I may have done. Wǒ kěnéng yǐjīng zuò dàole. 我可能已经做到了。

The beggar may have begged. Qǐgài kěnéng yǐjīng qǐtǎole. 乞丐可能已经乞讨了。

15 I might do. Wǒ kěnéng huì. 我可能会。

The beggar might beg. Qǐgài kěnéng huì qǐtǎo. 乞丐可能会乞讨。

16 I might be doing Wǒ kěnéng zhèngzài zuò 我可能正在做

The beggar might be begging. qǐgài kěnéng zài qǐtǎo. 乞丐可能在乞讨。

17 I must do. Wǒ bìxū zhèyàng zuò. 我必须这样做。

The beggar must beg. Qǐgài bìxū qǐtǎo. 乞丐必须乞讨。

18 I must be doing. Wǒ yīdìng shì zài zuò. 我一定是在做。

The beggar must be begging. Qǐgài yīdìng shì zài qǐtǎo. 乞丐一定是在乞讨。

19 I must have done. Wǒ yīdìng zuò dàole. 我一定做到了。

The beggar must have begged. Qǐgài yīdìng shì qǐtǎole. 乞丐一定是乞讨了。

20 I should do. Wǒ yīnggāi zuò. 我应该做。

The beggar should beg. Qǐgài yīnggāi qǐtǎo. 乞丐应该乞讨。

21 I should be doing. Wǒ yīnggāi zuò de. 我应该做的。

The beggar should be begging. Qǐgài yīnggāi qǐtǎo. 乞丐应该乞讨。

22 I should have done. Wǒ yīnggāi zuò de. 我应该做的。

The beggar should have begged. Qǐgài yīnggāi qǐtǎo. 乞丐应该乞讨。

23 I should have been doing. Wǒ yīnggāi yīzhí zài zuò. 我应该一直在做。

The beggar should have been begging. Qǐgài yīnggāi shì zài qǐtǎo. 乞丐应该是在乞讨。

24

The beggar used to beg. Qǐgài guòqù chángcháng qǐtǎo. 乞丐过去常常乞讨。

25 I am used to doing. / I am in the habit of doing. Wǒ xíguànle. / Wǒ yǒu zhèyàng zuò de xíguàn. 我习惯了。 / 我有这样做的习惯。

The beggar is used to begging. / The beggar is in the habit of begging. Qǐgài xíguàn yú qǐtǎo. / Qǐgài yǒu qǐtǎo de xíguàn. 乞丐习惯于乞讨。 / 乞丐有乞讨的习惯。

26 I was used to doing. / I was in the habit of doing. Wǒ yǐjīng xíguànle. / Wǒ yǒu zhèyàng zuò de xíguàn. 我已经习惯了。 / 我有这样做的习惯。

The beggar was used to begging. / The beggar was in the habit of begging. Qǐgài xíguàn yú qǐtǎo. / Qǐgài yǒu qǐtǎo de xíguàn. 乞丐习惯于乞讨。 / 乞丐有乞讨的习惯。

27 I am supposed to do. Wǒ yīnggāi zuò de. 我应该做的。

The beggar is supposed to beg. Qǐgài yīnggāi qǐtǎo. 乞丐**应该**乞讨。

28 I was supposed to do. Wǒ yīnggāi zuò de. 我**应该**做的。

The beggar was supposed to beg. Qǐgài běnlái yīnggāi qǐtǎo de. 乞丐本来**应该**乞讨的。

29 I have to do. Wǒ yào zuò. 我要做。

The beggar has to beg. Qǐgài bìxū qǐtǎo. 乞丐必须乞讨。

30 I had to do. Wǒ bìxū zuò. 我必须做。

The beggar had to beg. Qǐgài bùdé bù qǐtǎo. 乞丐不得不乞讨。

31 I have had to do. Wǒ bùdé bù zhèyàng zuò. 我不得不这样做。

The beggar have had to beg. Qǐgài bùdé bù qǐtǎo. 乞丐不得不乞讨。

32 I got to do. Wǒ dé zuò. 我得做。

The beggar got to beg. Qǐgài bùdé bù qǐtǎo. 乞丐不得不乞讨。

33 I got to be doing. Wǒ dé zuò. 我得做。

The beggar got to be begging. Qǐgài bìxū qǐtǎo. 乞丐必须乞讨。

34 I want you to do. Wǒ yào nǐ zuò. 我要你做。

I want the beggar to beg. Wǒ yào qǐgài qǐtǎo. 我要乞丐乞讨。

35 I wanted you to do. Wǒ xiǎng ràng nǐ zuò. 我想让你做。

I wanted the beggar to beg. Wǒ xiǎng ràng qǐgài qǐtǎo. 我想让乞丐乞讨。

36 You seem to do. Nǐ sìhū kěyǐ. 你似乎可以。

The beggar seems to beg. Qǐgài hǎoxiàng zài qǐtǎo. 乞丐好像在乞讨。

37 You seem to have done. Nǐ hǎoxiàng zuò dàole. 你好像做到了。

The beggar seems to have begged. Qǐgài hǎoxiàng qǐtǎole. 乞丐好像乞讨了。

38 You seemed to do. Nǐ sìhū zuò dàole. 你似乎做到了。

The beggar seemed to beg. Qǐgài sìhū zài qǐtǎo. 乞丐似乎在乞讨。

39 You seemed to have done. Nǐ hǎoxiàng zuò dàole. 你好像做到了。

The beggar seemed to have begged. Qǐgài sìhū shì zài qǐtǎo. 乞丐似乎是在乞讨。

40 I am able to do. Wǒ yǒu nénglì zuò dào. 我有能力做到。

The beggar is able to beg. Qǐgài kěyǐ qǐtǎo. 乞丐可以乞讨。

41 I was able to do. Wǒ nénggòu zuò dào. 我能够做到。

The beggar was able to beg. Qǐgài nénggòu qǐtǎo. 乞丐能够乞讨。

42 I am about to do. Wǒ zhèng yào zuò. 我正要做。

The beggar is about beg. Qǐgài shì guānyú qǐtǎo de. 乞丐是关于乞讨的。

43 I was about to do. Wǒ zhèng yào qù zuò. 我正要去做。

The beggar was about to beg. Qǐgài zhèng yào qǐtǎo. 乞丐正要乞讨。

44 I do do. Wǒ quèshí. 我确实。

The beggar do beg. Qǐgài qǐtǎo. 乞丐乞讨。

45 Let me do. Ràng wǒ zuò. 让我做。

Let the beggar beg. Ràng qǐgài qǐtǎo. 让乞丐乞讨。

46 Let me have to do. Ràng wǒ bùdé bù zuò. 让我不得不做。

Let the beggar have to beg. Ràng qǐgài bùdé bù qǐtǎo. 让乞丐不得不乞讨。

47 I try to do. Wǒ shìzhe qù zuò. 我试着去做。

The beggar tries to beg. Qǐgài shìtú qǐtǎo. 乞丐试图乞讨。

48 I tried to do. Wǒ shìzhe zuò. 我试着做。

The beggar tried to beg. Qǐgài shìtú qǐtǎo. 乞丐试图乞讨。

49 I love to do. Wǒ xǐhuān zuò. 我喜欢做。

The beggar loves to beg. Qǐgài xǐhuān qǐtǎo. 乞丐喜欢乞讨。

50 I loved to do. Wǒ xǐhuān zuò. 我喜欢做。

The beggar loved to beg. Qǐgài xǐhuān qǐtǎo. 乞丐喜欢乞讨。

51 I like to be doing. Wǒ xǐhuān zuò. 我喜欢做。

The beggar likes to be doing. Qǐgài xǐhuān zuò. 乞丐喜欢做。

52 I liked to be doing. Wǒ xǐhuān zuò. 我喜欢做。

The beggar liked to be begging. Qǐgài xǐhuān qǐtǎo. 乞丐喜欢乞讨。

53 I want to be doing. Wǒ xiǎng zuò. 我想做。

The beggar wants to be begging. Qǐgài xiǎng qǐtǎo. 乞丐想乞讨。

54 I wanted to be doing. Wǒ xiǎng zuò. 我想做。

The beggar wanted to be begging. Qǐgài xiǎng qǐtǎo. 乞丐想乞讨。

55 I like to do. Wǒ xǐhuān zuò. 我喜欢做。

The beggar likes to beg. Qǐgài xǐhuān qǐtǎo. 乞丐喜欢乞讨。

56 I liked to do. Wǒ xǐhuān zuò. 我喜欢做。

The beggar liked to beg. Qǐgài xǐhuān qǐtǎo. 乞丐喜欢乞讨。

57 I want to do. Wǒ xiǎng yào zuò. 我想要做。

The beggar wants to beg. Qǐgài xiǎng qǐtǎo. 乞丐想乞讨。

58 I wanted to do. Wǒ xiǎng zuò. 我想做。

The beggar wanted to beg. Qǐgài xiǎng qǐtǎo. 乞丐想乞讨。

59 I need to do. Wǒ xūyào qù zuò. 我需要去做。

The beggar needs to beg. Qǐgài xūyào qǐtǎo. 乞丐需要乞讨。

60 I needed to do. Wǒ xūyào zuò. 我需要做。

The beggar needed to beg. Qǐgài xūyào qǐtǎo. 乞丐需要乞讨。

61 I need to be doing. Wǒ xūyào zuò. 我需要做。

The beggar needs to be begging. Qǐgài xūyào qǐtǎo. 乞丐需要乞讨。

62 I needed to be doing. Wǒ xūyào zuò. 我需要做。

The beggar needed to be begging. Qǐgài xūyào qǐtǎo. 乞丐需要乞讨。

63 I hope to do. Wǒ xīwàng zuò dào. 我希望做到。

The beggar hopes to beg. Qǐgài xīwàng qǐtǎo. 乞丐希望乞讨。

64 I hoped to do. Wǒ xīwàng zhèyàng zuò. 我希望这样做。

The beggar hoped to beg. Qǐgài xīwàng qǐtǎo. 乞丐希望乞讨。

65 I dare to do. Wǒ gǎn zuò. 我敢做。

The beggar dares to beg. Qǐgài gǎn qǐtǎo. 乞丐敢乞讨。

66 I dared to do. Wǒ gǎn zuò. 我敢做。

The beggar dared to beg. Qǐgài gǎn qǐtǎo. 乞丐敢乞讨。

1 I don't do. Wǒ bù zuò. 我不做。

The baby doesn't sleep in the afternoon. Bǎobǎo xiàwǔ bù shuìjiào. 宝宝下午不睡觉。

2 I am not doing. Wǒ bùshì zài zuò. 我不是在做。

The baby isn't sleeping in the afternoon. Bǎobǎo xiàwǔ bù shuìjiào. 宝宝下午不睡觉。

3 I have not done. Wǒ méiyǒu zuòguò. 我没有做过。

The baby hasn't slept in the afternoon. Bǎobǎo xiàwǔ hái méi shuì. 宝宝下午还没睡。

4 I didn't do. Wǒ méiyǒu zuò. 我没有做。

The baby didn't sleep in the afternoon. Bǎobǎo xiàwǔ méi shuì. 宝宝下午没睡。

5 I was not doing. Wǒ bùshì zài zuò. 我不是在做。

The baby wasn't sleeping in the afternoon. Bǎobǎo xiàwǔ méi shuì. 宝宝下午没睡。

6 I will not do. Wǒ bù huì. 我不会。

The baby will not sleep in the afternoon. Bǎobǎo xiàwǔ bù shuìjiào. 宝宝下午不睡觉。

7 I will not be doing. Wǒ bù huì zuò de. 我不会做的。

The baby will not be sleeping in the afternoon. Bǎobǎo xiàwǔ bù shuìjiào. 宝宝下午不睡觉。

8 I will not have done. Wǒ bù huì zuò de. 我不会做的。

The baby will not have slept in the afternoon. Bǎobǎo xiàwǔ kěndìng shuì bùzháo. 宝宝下午肯定睡不着。

9 I can not do. Wǒ bùnéng zuò. 我不能做。

The baby can't sleep in the afternoon. Bǎobǎo xiàwǔshuì bùzháo. 宝宝下午睡不着。

10 I could not do. Wǒ zuò bù dào. 我做不到。

The baby couldn't sleep in the afternoon. Bǎobǎo xiàwǔ shuì bùzháo. 宝宝下午睡不着。

11 I could not have done. Wǒ zuò bù dào. 我做不到。

The baby couldn't have slept in the afternoon. Bǎobǎo xiàwǔ shuì bùzháo. 宝宝下午睡不着。

12 I may not do. Wǒ kěnéng bù huì. 我可能不会。

The baby may not sleep in the afternoon. Bǎobǎo xiàwǔ kěnéng shuì bùzháo. 宝宝下午可能睡不着。

13 I may not be doing. Wǒ kěnéng bù huì zuò. 我可能不会做。

The baby may not be sleeping in the afternoon. Bǎobǎo kěnéng zài xiàwǔ bù shuìjiào. 宝宝可能在下午不睡觉。

14 I may not have done. Wǒ kěnéng méiyǒu zuòguò. 我可能没有做过。

The baby may not have slept in the afternoon. Bǎobǎo xiàwǔ kěnéng méi shuì. 宝宝下午可能没睡。

15 I might not do. Wǒ kěnéng bù huì. 我可能不会。

The baby might not sleep in the afternoon. Bǎobǎo xiàwǔ kěnéng shuì bùzháo. 宝宝下午可能睡不着。

16 I might not be doing Wǒ kěnéng bù huì zuò 我可能不会做

The baby might not be sleeping in the afternoon. bǎobǎo xiàwǔ kěnéng bù shuìjiào. 宝宝下午可能不睡觉。

17 I must not do. Wǒ yīdìng bùnéng zhèyàng zuò. 我一定不能这样做。

The baby must not sleep in the afternoon. Bǎobǎo xiàwǔ yīdìng bùnéng shuìjiào. 宝宝下午一定不能睡觉。

18 I must not be doing. Wǒ yīdìng bùshì zài zuò. 我一定不是在做。

The baby must not be sleeping in the afternoon. Bǎobǎo bùnéng zài xiàwǔ shuìjiào. 宝宝不能在下午睡觉。

19 I must not have done. Wǒ yīdìng méiyǒu zuòguò. 我一定没有做过。

The baby must not have slept in the afternoon. Bǎobǎo xiàwǔ kěndìng méi shuì. 宝宝下午肯定没睡。

20 I should not do. Wǒ bù yìng gāi zhèyàng zuò. 我不应该这样做。

The baby shouldn't sleep in the afternoon. Bǎobǎo bù yìng gāi zài xiàwǔ shuìjiào. 宝宝不**应该**在下午睡**觉**。

21 I should not be doing. Wǒ bù yìng gāi zhèyàng zuò. 我不**应该**这样做。

The baby shouldn't be sleeping in the afternoon. Bǎobǎo bù yìng gāi zài xiàwǔ shuìjiào. 宝宝不**应该**在下午睡**觉**。

22 I should not have done. Wǒ bù yìng gāi zhèyàng zuò. 我不**应该**这样做。

The baby shouldn't have slept in the afternoon. Bǎobǎo xiàwǔ bù yìng gāi shuìjiào. 宝宝下午不**应该**睡**觉**。

23 I should not have been doing. Wǒ bù yìng gāi zhèyàng zuò. 我不**应该**这样做。

The baby shouldn't have been sleeping in the afternoon. Bǎobǎo bù yìng gāi zài xiàwǔ shuìjiào. 宝宝不**应该**在下午睡**觉**。

24 I didn't use to do. Wǒ méiyǒu zuò. 我没有做。

The baby didn't use to sleep in the afternoon. Bǎobǎo xiàwǔ bù xíguàn shuìjiào. 宝宝下午不**习惯**睡**觉**。

25 I am not used to doing. / I am in the habit of doing. Wǒ bù xíguàn zhèyàng zuò. / Wǒ yǒu zhèyàng zuò de xíguàn. 我不**习惯**这样做。 / 我有这样做的**习惯**。

The baby isn't used to sleeping in the afternoon. / The baby isn't in the habit of sleeping in the afternoon. Bǎobǎo bù xíguàn xiàwǔ shuìjiào. / Bǎobǎo méiyǒu wǔ shuì de xíguàn. 宝宝不**习惯**下午睡**觉**。 / 宝宝没有午睡的**习惯**。

26 I was not used to doing. / I was in the habit of doing. Wǒ bù xíguàn zhèyàng zuò. / Wǒ yǒu zhèyàng zuò de xíguàn. 我不**习惯**这样做。 / 我有这样做的**习惯**。

The baby wasn't used to sleeping in the afternoon. / The baby wasn't in the habit of sleeping in the afternoon. Bǎobǎo bù xíguàn xiàwǔ shuìjiào. / Bǎobǎo xiàwǔ méiyǒu shuìjiào de xíguàn. 宝宝不**习惯**下午睡**觉**。 / 宝宝下午没有睡**觉**的**习惯**。

27 I am not supposed to do. Wǒ bù yìng gāi zhèyàng zuò. 我不**应该**这样做。

The baby isn't supposed to sleep in the afternoon. Bǎobǎo xiàwǔ bù yìng gāi shuìjiào. 宝宝下午不**应该**睡**觉**。

28 I was not supposed to do. Wǒ bù yìng gāi zhèyàng zuò. 我不**应该**这样做。

The baby wasn't supposed to sleep in the afternoon. Bǎobǎo xiàwǔ bù yìng gāi shuìjiào. 宝宝下午不**应该**睡**觉**。

29 I don't have to do. Wǒ bùbì zhèyàng zuò. 我不必这样做。

The baby doesn't have to sleep in the afternoon. Bǎobǎo xiàwǔ bùyòng shuìjiào. 宝宝下午不用睡**觉**。

30 I didn't have to do. Wǒ bùbì zhèyàng zuò. 我不必这样做。

The baby didn't have to sleep in the afternoon. Bǎobǎo xiàwǔ bùyòng shuìjiào. 宝宝下午不用睡**觉**。

31 I don't have had to do. Wǒ bùbì zhèyàng zuò. 我不必这样做。

The baby doesn't have had to sleep in the afternoon. Bǎobǎo xiàwǔ bùyòng shuìjiào. 宝宝下午不用睡**觉**。

32 I didn't get to do. Wǒ méi dé zuò. 我没得做。

The baby didn't get to sleep in the afternoon. Bǎobǎo xiàwǔ méi shuì. 宝宝下午没睡。

33 I didn't get to be doing. Wǒ méiyǒu qù zuò. 我没有去做。

The baby didn't get to be sleeping in the afternoon. Bǎobǎo xiàwǔ shuì bùzháo. 宝宝下午睡不着。

34 I don't want you to do. Wǒ bù xīwàng nǐ zhèyàng zuò. 我不希望你这样做。

I don't want the baby to sleep in the afternoon. Wǒ bùxiǎng ràng bǎobǎo zài xiàwǔ shuìjiào. 我不想**让**宝宝在下午睡**觉**。

35 I didn't want you to do. Wǒ bùxiǎng ràng nǐ zhèyàng zuò. 我不想**让**你这样做。

I didn't want the baby to sleep in the afternoon. Wǒ bùxiǎng ràng bǎobǎo zài xiàwǔ shuìjiào. 我不想**让**宝宝在下午睡**觉**。

36 You don't seem to do. Nǐ sìhū méiyǒu. 你似乎没有。

The baby doesn't seem to sleep in the afternoon. Bǎobǎo xiàwǔ hǎoxiàng méi shuì. 宝宝下午好像没睡。

37 You don't seem to have done. Nǐ sìhū méiyǒu zuò dào. 你似乎没有做到。

The baby doesn't seem to have slept in the afternoon. Bǎobǎo xiàwǔ hǎoxiàng méi shuì. 宝宝下午好像没睡。

38 You didn't seem to do. Nǐ hǎoxiàng méiyǒu. 你好像没有。

The baby didn't seem to sleep in the afternoon. Bǎobǎo xiàwǔ hǎoxiàng méi shuì. 宝宝下午好像没睡。

39 You didn't seem to have done. Nǐ sìhū méiyǒu zuò dào. 你似乎没有做到。

The baby didn't seem to have slept in the afternoon. Bǎobǎo xiàwǔ hǎoxiàng méi shuì. 宝宝下午好像没睡。

40 I am not able to do. Wǒ zuò bù dào. 我做不到。

The baby isn't able to sleep in the afternoon. Bǎobǎo xiàwǔ shuì bùzháo. 宝宝下午睡不着。

41 I was not able to do. Wǒ méi néng zuò dào. 我没能做到。

The baby wasn't able to sleep in the afternoon. Bǎobǎo xiàwǔ shuì bùzháo. 宝宝下午睡不着。

42 I am not about to do. Wǒ bù dǎsuàn zuò. 我不打算做。

The baby isn't about to sleep in the afternoon. Bǎobǎo xiàwǔ bù shuìjiào. 宝宝下午不睡觉。

43 I was not about to do. Wǒ bù dǎsuàn zuò. 我不打算做。

The baby wasn't about to sleep in the afternoon. Bǎobǎo xiàwǔ bù shuìjiào. 宝宝下午不睡觉。

44 I do never do. Wǒ cóng bù zhèyàng zuò. 我从不这样做。

The baby does never sleep in the afternoon. Bǎobǎo xiàwǔ cóng bù shuìjiào. 宝宝下午从不睡觉。

45 Don't let me do. Bùyào ràng wǒ zuò. 不要让我做。

Don't let the baby sleep in the afternoon. Xiàwǔ bùyào ràng bǎobǎo shuìjiào. 下午不要让宝宝睡觉。

46 Don't let me have to do. Bùyào ràng wǒ bùdé bù zuò. 不要让我不得不做。

Don't let the baby have to sleep in the afternoon. Xiàwǔ bùyào ràng bǎobǎo shuìjiào. 下午不要让宝宝睡觉。

47 I don't try to do. / I try not to do. Wǒ bù chángshì qù zuò. / Wǒ jǐnliàng bù zuò. 我不尝试去做。 / 我尽量不做。

The baby doesn't try to sleep in the afternoon. / The baby try not to sleep in the afternoon. Bǎobǎo xiàwǔ bùxiǎng shuìjiào. / Bǎobǎo jǐnliàng bùyào zài xiàwǔ shuìjiào. 宝宝下午不想睡觉。 / 宝宝尽量不要在下午睡觉。

48 I didn't try to do. / I tried not to do. Wǒ méiyǒu chángshì qù zuò. / Wǒ shìzhe bù zhèyàng zuò. 我没有尝试去做。 / 我试着不这样做。

The baby didn't try to sleep in the afternoon. / The baby tried not to sleep in the afternoon. Bǎobǎo xiàwǔ bùxiǎng shuìjiào. / Bǎobǎo xiàwǔ jǐnliàng bù shuìjiào. 宝宝下午不想睡觉。 /宝宝下午尽量不睡觉。

49 I don't love to do. Wǒ bù xǐhuān zuò. 我不喜欢做。

The baby doesn't love to sleep in the afternoon. Bǎobǎo bù xǐhuān zài xiàwǔ shuìjiào. 宝宝不喜欢在下午睡觉。

50 I didn't love to do. Wǒ bù xǐhuān zuò. 我不喜欢做。

The baby didn't love to sleep in the afternoon. Bǎobǎo bù xǐhuān zài xiàwǔ shuìjiào. 宝宝不喜欢在下午睡觉。

51 I don't like to be doing. Wǒ bù xǐhuān zuò. 我不喜欢做。

The baby doesn't like to be sleeping in the afternoon. Bǎobǎo bù xǐhuān zài xiàwǔ shuìjiào. 宝宝不喜欢在下午睡觉。

52 I didn't like to be doing. Wǒ bù xǐhuān zuò. 我不喜欢做。

The baby didn't like to be sleeping in the afternoon. Bǎobǎo bù xǐhuān zài xiàwǔ shuìjiào. 宝宝不喜欢在下午睡觉。

53 I don't want to be doing. Wǒ bùxiǎng zuò. 我不想做。

The baby doesn't want to be sleeping in the afternoon. Bǎobǎo bùxiǎng zài xiàwǔ shuìjiào. 宝宝不想在下午睡觉。

54 I didn't want to be doing. Wǒ bùxiǎng zuò. 我不想做。

The baby didn't want to be sleeping in the afternoon. Bǎobǎo xiàwǔ bùxiǎng shuìjiào. 宝宝下午不想睡觉。

55 I don't like to do. Wǒ bù xǐhuān zuò. 我不喜欢做。

The baby doesn't like to sleep in the afternoon. Bǎobǎo bù xǐhuān zài xiàwǔ shuìjiào. 宝宝不喜欢在下午睡觉。

56 I didn't like to do. Wǒ bù xǐhuān zuò. 我不喜欢做。

The baby didn't like to sleep in the afternoon. Bǎobǎo xiàwǔ bù xǐhuān shuìjiào. 宝宝下午不喜欢睡觉。

57 I don't want to do. Wǒ bùxiǎng zuò. 我不想做。

The baby doesn't want to sleep in the afternoon. Bǎobǎo xiàwǔ bùxiǎng shuìjiào. 宝宝下午不想睡觉。

58 I didn't want to do. Wǒ bùxiǎng zuò. 我不想做。

The baby didn't want sleep in the afternoon. Bǎobǎo xiàwǔ bùxiǎng shuìjiào. 宝宝下午不想睡觉。

59 I don't need to do. Wǒ bù xūyào zuò. 我不需要做。

The baby doesn't need to sleep in the afternoon. Bǎobǎo xiàwǔ bù xūyào shuìjiào. 宝宝下午不需要睡觉。

60 I didn't need to do. Wǒ bù xūyào zuò. 我不需要做。

The baby didn't need to sleep in the afternoon. Bǎobǎo xiàwǔ bù xūyào shuìjiào. 宝宝下午不需要睡觉。

61 I don't need to be doing. Wǒ bù xūyào zuò. 我不需要做。

The baby doesn't need to be sleeping in the afternoon. Bǎobǎo xiàwǔ bù xūyào shuìjiào. 宝宝下午不需要睡觉。

62 I didn't need to be doing. Wǒ bù xūyào zuò. 我不需要做。

The baby didn't need to be sleeping in the afternoon. Bǎobǎo xiàwǔ bù xūyào shuìjiào. 宝宝下午不需要睡觉。

63 I don't hope to do. Wǒ bù xīwàng zhèyàng zuò. 我不希望这样做。

The baby doesn't hope to sleep in the afternoon. Bǎobǎo bù xīwàng xiàwǔ shuìjiào. 宝宝不希望下午睡觉。

64 I didn't hope to do. Wǒ bù xīwàng zhèyàng zuò. 我不希望这样做。

The baby didn't hope to sleep in the afternoon. Bǎobǎo bù xīwàng xiàwǔ shuìjiào. 宝宝不希望下午睡觉。

65 I don't dare to do. Wǒ bù gǎn zuò. 我不敢做。

The baby doesn't dare to sleep in the afternoon. Bǎobǎo xiàwǔ bù gǎn shuìjiào. 宝宝下午不敢睡觉。

66 I didn't dare to do. Wǒ bù gǎn zuò. 我不敢做。

The baby didn't dare to sleep in the afternoon. Bǎobǎo xiàwǔ bù gǎn shuìjiào. 宝宝下午不敢睡觉。

1 Do I do? Wǒ zuò ma? 我做吗？

Does the farmers plough in the field? Nóngmín zài dì lǐ lí dì ma? 农民在地里犁地吗？

2 AM I doing? Wǒ zài zuò shénme? 我在做什么？

Are the farmers ploughing in the field? Nóngmínmen zài tián lǐ lí dì ma? 农民们在田里犁地吗？

3 Have I done? Wǒ zuò dàole ma? 我做到了吗？

4 Did I do? Wǒ zuòle ma? 我做了吗？

5 Was I doing? Wǒ zài zuò shénme? 我在做什么？

6 Will I do? Wǒ huì zuò ma? 我会做吗？

7 Will I be doing? Wǒ huì zuò ma? 我会做吗？

8 Will I have done? Wǒ huì zuò ma? 我会做吗？

9 Can I do? Wǒ kěbù kěyǐ zuò? 我可不可以做？

10 Could I do? Wǒ kěyǐ ma? 我可以吗？

11 Could I have done? Wǒ néng zuò dào ma? 我能做到吗？

12 May I do? Wǒ kěyǐ ma? 我可以吗？

13 May I be doing? Wǒ kěyǐ zài zuò shénme ma? 我可以在做什么吗？

14 May I have done? Wǒ kěyǐ zuò ma? 我可以做吗？

15 Might I do? Wǒ kěyǐ ma? 我可以吗？

16 Might I be doing? Wǒ kěnéng zài zuò shénme? 我可能在做什么？

17 Must I do? Wǒ bìxū zhèyàng zuò ma? 我必须这样做吗？

18 Must I be doing? Wǒ bìxū zuò ma? 我必须做吗？

19 Must I have done? Wǒ bìxū zuò ma? 我必须做吗？

20 Should I do? Wǒ yīnggāi zuò ma? 我应该做吗？

21 Should I be doing? Wǒ yīnggāi zuò shénme? 我应该做什么？

22 Should I have done? Wǒ yīnggāi zuò ma? 我应该做吗？

23 Should I have been doing? Wǒ yīnggāi yīzhí zài zuò shénme? 我应该一直在做什么？

24 Did I use to do? Wǒ yǐqián zuòguò ma? 我以前做过吗？

25 AM I used to doing? / Am I in the habit of doing? Wǒ xíguànle ma? / Wǒ yǒu zhèyàng zuò de xíguàn ma? 我习惯了吗？ / 我有这样做的习惯吗？

26 Was I used to doing? / Was I in the habit of doing? Wǒ xíguànle ma? / Wǒ yǒu zhèyàng zuò de xíguàn ma? 我习惯了吗？ / 我有这样做的习惯吗？

27 AM I supposed to do? Wǒ yīnggāi zěnme zuò? 我应该怎么做？

28 Was I supposed to do? Wǒ yīnggāi zěnme zuò? 我应该怎么做？

29 Do I have to do? Wǒ bìxū zhèyàng zuò ma? 我必须这样做吗？

30 Did I have to do? Wǒ bìxū zhèyàng zuò ma? 我必须这样做吗？

31 Do I have had to do? Wǒ bùdé bù zhèyàng zuò ma? 我不得不这样做吗？

32 Did I get to do? Wǒ yǒu zuò ma? 我有做吗？

33 Did I get to be doing? Wǒ yǒu zuòshì ma? 我有做事吗？

34 Do I want you to do? Wǒ yào nǐ zuò shénme? 我要你做什么？

35 Did I want you to do? Wǒ xiǎng ràng nǐ zuò ma? 我想让你做吗？

36 Do you seem to do? Nǐ hǎoxiàng ne? 你好像呢？

37 Do you seem to have done? Nǐ hǎoxiàng zuò dàole? 你好像做到了？

38 Did you seem to do? Nǐ hǎoxiàng zuò dàole? 你好像做到了？

39 Did you seem to have done? Nǐ hǎoxiàng zuò dàole? 你好像做到了？

40 AM I able to do? Wǒ néng zuò dào ma? 我能做到吗？

41 Was I able to do? Wǒ néng zuò dào ma? 我能做到吗？

42 AM I about to do? Wǒ yào zuò ma? 我要做吗？

43 Was I about to do? Wǒ yào zuò ma? 我要做吗？

44 Do I do do? Wǒ zuò ma? 我做吗？

45

46

47 Do I try to do? Wǒ chángshì zuò ma? 我尝试做吗？

48 Did I try to do? Wǒ shìguò ma? 我试过吗？

49 Do I love to do? Wǒ xǐhuān zuò ma? 我喜欢做吗？

50 Did I love to do? Wǒ xǐhuān zuò ma? 我喜欢做吗？

51 Do I like to be doing? Wǒ xǐhuān zuòshì ma? 我喜欢做事吗？

52 Did I like to be doing? Wǒ xǐhuān zuò ma? 我喜欢做吗？

53 Do I want to be doing? Wǒ xiǎng zuò ma? 我想做吗？

54 Did I want to be doing? Wǒ xiǎng zuò ma? 我想做吗？

55 Do I like to do? Wǒ xǐhuān zuò shénme? 我喜欢做什么？

56 Did I like to do? Wǒ xǐhuān zuò ma? 我喜欢做吗？

57 Do I want to do? Wǒ xiǎng zuò ma? 我想做吗？

58 Did I want to do? Wǒ xiǎng zuò ma? 我想做吗？

59 Do I need to do? Wǒ xūyào zuò ma? 我需要做吗？

60 Did I need to do? Wǒ xūyào zuò ma? 我需要做吗？

61 Do I need to be doing? Wǒ xūyào zuò ma? 我需要做吗？

62 Did I need to be doing? Wǒ xūyào zuò ma? 我需要做吗？

63 Do I hope to do? Wǒ xīwàng zhèyàng zuò ma? 我希望这样做吗？

64 Did I hope to do? Wǒ xīwàng zhèyàng zuò ma? 我希望这样做吗？

65 Do I dare to do? Wǒ gǎn zuò ma? 我敢做吗？

66 Did I dare to do? Wǒ gǎn zuò ma? 我敢做吗？

1 Do I not do? Wǒ bù zuò ma? 我不做吗？

Does the farmers not plough in the field? Nóngmín bù gēng tián ma? 农民不耕田吗？

2 AM I not doing? Wǒ bùshì zài zuò ma? 我不是在做吗？

3 Have I not done? Wǒ méiyǒu zuò ma? 我没有做吗？

4 Did I not do? Wǒ méiyǒu zuò ma? 我没有做吗？

5 Was I not doing? Wǒ bùshì zài zuò ma? 我不是在做吗？

6 Will I not do? Wǒ bù huì ma? 我不会吗？

7 Will I not be doing? Wǒ bù huì zuò ma? 我不会做吗？

8 Will I not have done? Wǒ bù huì zuò ma? 我不会做吗？

9 Can I not do? Wǒ kěyǐ bù zuò ma? 我可以不做吗？

10 Could I not do? Wǒ kěyǐ bù zuò ma? 我可以不做吗？

11 Could I not have done? Wǒ kěyǐ bù zuò ma? 我可以不做吗？

12 May I not do? Wǒ kěyǐ bù zuò ma? 我可以不做吗？

13 May I not be doing? Wǒ kěyǐ bù zuò ma? 我可以不做吗？

14 May I not have done? Wǒ kěnéng méiyǒu zuòguò ma? 我可能没有做过吗？

15 Might I not do? Wǒ kěyǐ bù zuò ma? 我可以不做吗？

16 Might I not be doing? Wǒ kěyǐ bù zuò ma? 我可以不做吗？

17 Must I not do? Wǒ bìxū bù zhèyàng zuò ma? 我必须不这样做吗？

18 Must I not be doing? Wǒ bìxū bù zuò ma? 我必须不做吗？

19 Must I not have done? Wǒ yīdìng méiyǒu zuòguò ma? 我一定没有做过吗？

20 Should I not do? Wǒ bù yìng gāi zuò ma? 我不应该做吗？

21 Should I not be doing? Wǒ bù yìng gāi zuò ma? 我不应该做吗？

22 Should I not have done? Wǒ bù yìng gāi zuò ma? 我不应该做吗？

23 Should I not have been doing? Wǒ bù yìng gāi yīzhí zài zuò ma? 我不应该一直在做吗？

24 Did I not use to do? Wǒ méi yòngguò ma? 我没用过吗？

25 AM I not used to doing? / Am I not in the habit of doing? Wǒ bù xíguàn ma? / Wǒ méiyǒu zhèyàng zuò de xíguàn ma? 我不习惯吗？ / 我没有这样做的习惯吗？

26 Was I not used to doing? / Was I not in the habit of doing? Shì wǒ bù xíguàn ma? / Nándào wǒ méiyǒu zhèyàng zuò de xíguàn? 是我不习惯吗？ / 难道我没有这样做的习惯？

27 AM I not supposed to do? Wǒ bù yìng gāi zhèyàng zuò ma? 我不应该这样做吗？

28 Was I not supposed to do? Wǒ bùshì yīnggāi zuò de ma? 我不是应该做的吗？

29 Do I not have to do? Nándào wǒ bùyòng ma? 难道我不用吗？

30 Did I not have to do? Wǒ bùshì bìxū zuò ma? 我不是必须做吗？

31 Do I not have had to do? Nándào wǒ méiyǒu bànfǎ ma? 难道我没有办法吗？

32 Did I not get to do? Wǒ méiyǒu zuò ma? 我没有做吗？

33 Did I not get to be doing? Wǒ méiyǒu zuò ma? 我没有做吗？

34 Do I not want you to do? Wǒ bùxiǎng nǐ zuò shénme? 我不想你做什么？

35 Did I not want you to do? Wǒ bùshì yào nǐ zuò ma? 我不是要你做吗？

36 Do you not seem to do? Hǎoxiàng bù zuò ma? 好像不做吗？

37 Do you not seem to have done? Hǎoxiàng méiyǒu zuò ma? 好像没有做吗？

38 Did you not seem to do? Nǐ hǎoxiàng méi zuò? 你好像没做？

39 Did you not seem to have done? Nǐ hǎoxiàng méi zuòguò? 你好像没做过？

40 AM I not able to do? Wǒ zuò bù dào ma? 我做不到吗？

41 Was I not able to do? Wǒ zuò bù dào ma? 我做不到吗？

42 AM I not about to do? Wǒ bù zhǔnbèi zuò ma? 我不准备做吗？

43 Was I not about to do? Wǒ bùshì yào zuò shénme ma? 我不是要做什么吗？

44 Do I do never do? Wǒ cónglái bu zuò ma? 我从来不做吗？

45

46

47 Do I not try to do? Nándào wǒ bù shì shì ma? 难道我不试试吗？

48 Did I not try to do? Wǒ méiyǒu chángshì zuò ma? 我没有尝试做吗？

49 Do I not love to do? Nándào wǒ bù ài zuò ma? 难道我不爱做吗？

50 Did I not love to do? Wǒ bù ài zuò ma? 我不爱做吗？

51 Do I not like to be doing? Wǒ bù xǐhuān bèi zuò ma? 我不喜欢被做吗？

52 Did I not like to be doing? Wǒ bù xǐhuān zuò ma? 我不喜欢做吗？

53 Do I not want to be doing? Wǒ bùxiǎng zuò ma? 我不想做吗？

54 Did I not want to be doing? Wǒ bùxiǎng zuò ma? 我不想做吗？

55 Do I not like to do? Wǒ bù xǐhuān zuò shénme? 我不喜欢做什么？

56 Did I not like to do? Wǒ bù xǐhuān zuò ma? 我不喜欢做吗？

57 Do I not want to do? Wǒ bùxiǎng zuò ma? 我不想做吗？

58 Did I not want to do? Wǒ bùxiǎng zuò ma? 我不想做吗？

59 Do I not need to do? Wǒ bù xūyào zuò ma? 我不需要做吗？

60 Did I not need to do? Wǒ bù xūyào zuò ma? 我不需要做吗？

61 Do I not need to be doing? Wǒ bù xūyào zuò ma? 我不需要做吗？

62 Did I not need to be doing? Wǒ bù xūyào zuò ma? 我不需要做吗？

63 Do I not hope to do? Nándào wǒ bù xīwàng ma? 难道我不希望吗？

64 Did I not hope to do? Nándào wǒ méiyǒu xīwàng ma? 难道我没有希望吗？

65 Do I dare to do? Wǒ gǎn zuò ma? 我敢做吗？

66 Did I not dare to do? Wǒ bù gǎn zuò ma? 我不敢做吗？

https://www.coursera.org/learn/learn-chinese/home/welcome

www.ingramcontent.com/pod-product-compliance
Ingram Content Group UK Ltd.
Pitfield, Milton Keynes, MK11 3LW, UK
UKHW021918190726
13853UKWH00002B/725

9 798885 469937